8.50 mc
no

D1617023

SIX LECTURES

ON THE

ANTE-NICENE FATHERS.

SIX LECTURES

ON THE

ANTE-NICENE FATHERS

BY

FENTON JOHN ANTHONY HORT

Essay Index Reprint Series

 BOOKS FOR LIBRARIES PRESS
FREEPORT, NEW YORK

First Published 1895
Reprinted 1972

Library of Congress Cataloging in Publication Data

Hort, Fenton John Anthony, 1828-1892.
    Six lectures on the ante-Nicene fathers.

    (Essay index reprint series)
    Reprint of the 1895 ed.
    CONTENTS: Clement of Rome and Hermas.--Ignatius
and Polycarp.--Justin and Irenaeus. ⌐etc.⌐
    1. Fathers of the church. 2. Apostolic Fathers.
I. Title.
BR1705.H8 1972   281'.3'0922 ⌐B⌐   79-37789
ISBN 0-8369-2596-3

PRINTED IN THE UNITED STATES OF AMERICA
BY
NEW WORLD BOOK MANUFACTURING CO., INC.
HALLANDALE, FLORIDA 33009

PREFATORY NOTE.

THESE lectures were delivered by my father to the Clergy Training School at Cambridge in the Lent Term of 1890.

They are almost the only popular lectures which he gave : they are of a widely different character from his other lectures on Church History now in course of publication, and will appeal perhaps to a rather wider circle of readers. Though popular in treatment, they were however composed with all Dr Hort's accustomed care : he had had some idea of revising them for publication. The text of each lecture was written out in full, and the illustrative extracts from the works of the Fathers were read in translations partly published, partly of his own making : these characteristic specimens of writers of whose permanent value he was strongly convinced, will, it is hoped, be found not the least useful part of the volume, such a collection of passages not being easily accessible elsewhere. There is some uncertainty as to the limits of one of the passages quoted, that from Justin Martyr, but I hope that those here printed are substantially the extracts read in the course of each lecture. The quotations from Clement, Ignatius and Polycarp are taken from Bishop Lightfoot's *Apostolic Fathers*, that from Justin Martyr from the Rev. G. Reith's translation in the "Ante-Nicene Christian Library," with some alterations adopted from pencilled notes in Dr Hort's copy: for the two passages from Origen I am responsible, and have made use of the Rev. Dr Crombie's version in the same series: I could not discover whether the lecturer here used any published or manuscript translation. The two extracts from Irenæus were transcribed by Dr Hort himself.

A. F. HORT.

CONTENTS.

LECTURE I.

CLEMENT OF ROME AND HERMAS.

THE lectures which I hope to deliver this term are intended to have for their subject "Some early Fathers of the Church." In this description of the proposed subject the word "Fathers" means simply what it means in common usage, the Christian writers of the early Christian centuries. In one literal sense they might be called Fathers, viz. as being the parents of the Christian thought and belief and life of later centuries, which, however modified and altered by the inward and outward changes arising in the course of time, retain always down to the present day important features inherited from the peculiar circumstances of the centuries which followed the Apostolic age.

But, although it is important to remember that our own thoughts, and the thoughts of all

Christians everywhere, have been in a great measure thus shaped for us by the thoughts of the early Fathers, it is not on account of this fact that we call them Fathers, but rather in gratitude and veneration for them as the patriarchs of Christendom, speaking to us still out of that early dawn of the Christian period of history, and often speaking to us out of the fiery trial of persecution. But it would be a misuse of this legitimate reverence to treat the words of the Fathers as oracles appointed to dictate to us what we ought to believe. If we read their words with an open and teachable mind, we shall often find there abundant help and instruction, but the responsibility will always lie upon us of weighing and testing what we read, to the best of our power. We must not be surprised if we sometimes find much dross, for each age has its own limitations and vagaries, and, besides these, each man in each age has his own limitations and vagaries, some more, some less.

Again it is not really possible to measure the comparative worth of the Fathers, one with another, merely by their comparative antiquity. There is no doubt a peculiar freshness in the best writings of quite the earliest time, the only time which can with any propriety share with the Apostolic Age the much misused and slippery epithet "primitive." But the greatest of the Fathers belong to later times, and different later times, when in doctrine and in institutions and in various other things pertaining to Christian life, great and unavoidable changes had taken place, changes that were on the whole for good and belonging to healthy growth, but also by no means free from loss, from injurious onesided-ness, and from corruption. In what we call the age of the Fathers there was anything rather than a uniform state of things. Movement was at that time more rapid than probably at any later time of Christian history.

There are several comparatively distinct subjects which might properly enough be lec-tured about or written about in connexion with the Fathers. They might serve as a thread for speaking about Church History generally, or about the History of doctrine, of course in either case within the limits of their own time. Or again they might, with more obvious fitness, be taken as the heads of the corre-sponding history of Christian literature. The time at our disposal will not however allow us to follow any of these lines, unless it be incidentally and to a small extent. I wish rather to do what I can towards putting before you the leading Fathers of the earliest centuries as living men, the children of a particular time, and to give some account of the purpose and character of their chief works, illustrated by translated extracts which may help towards the formation of individual impressions that may remain associated with their respective names.

It is well to keep in mind throughout that only a small part of the actual Christian literature of the early centuries is now preserved to us. Not only many books, but all the books of many authors, have completely perished. Of others we possess only scanty fragments. On the other hand, when we observe the neglect or even dislike with which the Ante-Nicene Christian literature, with very limited exceptions, was regarded by most of the Christian theologians of later days, we can hardly be too thankful that so much has been preserved; and moreover that what has been preserved has so representative a character, that is, supplies us with substantial and important examples of

different times, different schools, and different
churches. Again it is a striking and encouraging fact that so many lost works, or lost portions
of works, belonging to this period have come to
light within the last forty years. Nor is there
any reason to believe that we have come to the
end of discoveries of this kind.

The Fathers of whom I propose to speak
to-day belong to the small group to which it has
been usual for above two hundred years to give
the rather unmeaning name Apostolic Fathers,
that is, preeminently Clement of Rome, Hermas,
Ignatius, and Polycarp. In the opinion of many
the earliest extant Christian writing outside the
New Testament is the remarkable little manual
of Christian morals and ecclesiastical instruction
calling itself the Teaching of the Twelve Apostles, now familiarly known as the Didache,
which was discovered and published a few years
ago. It may however be considerably later :
and at all events it lies too near the edge of our
subject to need more than this passing word of
notice.

We begin then with Clement of Rome. The
little that is really known about him will be best
found in Dr Lightfoot's admirable edition, and

still more in the Appendix which he published
eight years later, in which he has carefully sifted
the mass of ancient legend and modern specula-
tion which has gathered round Clement's name.
Some pages of his Philippians are also worth
reading in the same connexion.   The apparent
time when the Epistle was written and the
apparent personal position of Clement are both
remarkable.   Some thirty years had passed, what
is counted a generation, since the persecution of
Nero, some twenty-five years since the fall of
Jerusalem, the greatest as well as most awful of
events for all Christians.   For the Empire, after
all the frightful turmoil which had followed the
death of Nero, a happier time had already begun
with the accession of Vespasian, a period Dr Meri-
vale says "distinguished by the general prosperity
of the administration, the tranquil obedience of
the people, and (with a single exception) by the
virtue and public spirit of the rulers." Vespasian's
son Titus had succeeded, and then his other son
Domitian, his reign being the one exception to
the comparative brightness of the series of eight.
Always capricious and suspicious, the emperor
shewed these qualities in an extreme form about
the years A.D. 95, 96, the last of his life.   Among

his victims were his own first cousin and niece's husband, Flavius Clemens, the father of the two reputed heirs to the empire. This Clemens was executed, and his wife exiled, both apparently as having become Christians. The Clement who wrote our Epistle was, it would seem, a freedman or freedman's son in their household, and had in this manner received his name. Everything in his letter shews that he must have been long a Christian himself, so that his mind would naturally be saturated, as we find it, with the language and ideas of the Old Testament, the only Scriptures, properly so called, for Christians at this early time, even if he was not previously, as is possible, a Jew of the Dispersion. His precise position in the Roman Church is difficult to ascertain. Two or three generations later, when the early constitution of the European Churches had been forgotten, he was placed in the series of early Bishops of Rome. But, as Dr Lightfoot has shewn (Phil. p. 218, ed. 8), it is difficult to reconcile his holding such an office with the language of the Epistle itself, or with other indications as to the constitution of the Church of Rome at a somewhat later time. But he must certainly have been a man of importance and influence in the Church to be entrusted with the duty of writing such an Epistle, even if he was not the Clement to whom the book of Hermas' Visions (to which we shall come shortly) was to be sent for sending on to the cities away from Rome, that task, it is said, having been entrusted to him.

The Epistle itself starts with a salutation resembling those of the Apostolic Epistles, beginning "The Church of God which sojourns at Rome to the Church of God which sojourns at Corinth." The first words of the letter itself shew the state of things at Rome. "Because of the sudden and quickly succeeding misfortunes and calamities happening to us, brethren, we deem that we have been somewhat slow in giving attention to the matters that are in dispute among you." Thus the Epistle was written during or soon after the persecution which fell on the Roman Christians in those last months of Domitian's reign, the first persecution of which we have any knowledge after the persecution of Nero and the immediately following time of confusion.

The purpose of this the first extant writing

of a Christian Father is the promotion of peace,
the restoration of a divided and disorderly
Christian community to the concord and order
implied in the very idea of Church-membership.
At the outset the Roman Church commends
warmly the previous temper and conduct shewn
by the Corinthian Church, and then especially
those ways of theirs to which the present state
of things stood in the strongest contrast[1]. In
place of all this had now come what is called
(1) a vile and unholy sedition (or quarrel, στάσις),
kindled by a few headlong and self-willed persons
to a pitch of madness which had brought their
honourable name into disgrace. It had arisen,
we read further on, from contumacy shewn
against some of the elders of the Church, who
had been thrust aside without having deserved
it (44, 47, 57, etc.). This conduct is traced back
(3 fin.) to "an unrighteous and impious jealousy"
(ζῆλος), a jealousy of which examples are given
as leading to great crimes and misfortunes in the
times of the Old Testament, and now again as
leading to the martyr deaths of Peter and Paul
and many others of those who are called "elect."
These admonitions the Roman Church then

[1] Lightfoot, *Clement of Rome*, Appendix, p. 346.

takes up as addressed equally to themselves:
" we are in the same arena, and the same contest
awaits us." "Let us hearken (9) to His majestic
and glorious purpose, and coming as suppliants
of His mercy and graciousness let us fall down
[before Him] and turn to His compassions,
abandoning the labouring that is vain and the
strife and the jealousy that leads to death."
Then follow examples of those "who have
ministered perfectly to God's majestic glory" by
obedience or faith or in other like ways, beginning with Enoch, Noah, and Abraham, the words
of the Old Testament being copiously cited as
well as the lives of its holy men.

" The humility therefore and the submissive-
ness of so many and so great men, who have
thus obtained a good report, hath through
obedience made better not only us but also the
generations which were before us, even them
that received His oracles in fear and truth.
Seeing then that we have been partakers of
many great and glorious doings, let us hasten
to return unto the goal of peace which hath
been handed down to us from the beginning,
and let us look steadfastly unto the Father and
Maker of the whole world, and cleave unto His

splendid and excellent gifts of peace and
benefits.   Let us behold Him in our mind, and
let us look with the eyes of our soul unto His
long-suffering will.   Let us note how free from
anger He is towards all His creatures.

"The heavens are moved by His direction
and obey Him in peace.   Day and night accomplish the course assigned to them by Him,
without hindrance one to another.   Moreover,
the inscrutable depths of the abysses and the
unutterable statutes of the nether regions are
constrained by the same ordinances.   The basin
of the boundless sea, gathered together by His
workmanship into its reservoirs, passeth not the
barriers wherewith it is surrounded ; but even
as He ordered it, so it doeth.   For He said,
'So far shalt thou come, and thy waves shall be
broken within thee.'   The ocean which is im-
passable for men, and the worlds beyond it, are
directed by the same ordinances of the Master.
The seasons of spring and summer and autumn
and winter give way in succession one to another
in peace.   The winds in their several quarters
at their proper season fulfil their ministry without disturbance ; and the ever-flowing fountains,
created for enjoyment and health, without fail

give their breasts which sustain the life of men. Yea, the smallest of living things come together in concord and peace. All these things the great Creator and Master of the universe ordered to be in peace and concord, doing good unto all things, but far beyond the rest unto us who have taken refuge in His compassionate mercies through our Lord Jesus Christ, to whom be the glory and the majesty for ever and ever. Amen[1]."

Then follows a series of chapters of religious exhortation in the same lofty strain, ending with texts thus introduced.

"This is the way, dearly-beloved, wherein we found our salvation, even Jesus Christ the High-priest of our offerings, the Guardian and Helper of our weakness. Through Him let us look steadfastly unto the heights of the heavens ; through Him we behold as in a mirror His faultless and most excellent visage ; through Him the eyes of our hearts were opened; through Him our foolish and darkened mind springeth up unto the light ; through Him the Master willeth that we should taste of the immortal knowledge ; 'Who being the brightness of His

---

[1] Lightfoot, *Clement of Rome*, Appendix, pp. 355 foll.

majesty is so much greater than angels, as He
hath inherited a more excellent name.' For so
it is written; 'Who maketh His angels spirits
and His ministers a flame of fire'; but of His
Son the Master said thus; 'Thou art my Son,
I this day have begotten Thee. Ask of me,
and I will give Thee the Gentiles for Thine
inheritance, and the ends of the earth for Thy
possession.' And again He saith unto Him;
'Sit thou on My right hand, until I make Thine
enemies a footstool for Thy feet.' Who then
are these enemies? They that are wicked and
resist His will[1]."

The original subject of the Epistle returns in
a fresh exposition of the necessity and Divine-
ness of order.

"The great without the small cannot exist,
neither the small without the great" (according
to the wise Greek proverb). "All the members
breathe together and join in one [common] subjection that the whole body may be saved."
This spirit of order is traced in the Mosaic
legislation, and in the office and work of the
apostles who received the Gospel for us from
Jesus Christ, even as He was sent forth from

[1] Lightfoot, *Clement of Rome*, Appendix, p. 364.

God. The details of what is said about the appointments of elders or men having oversight by the Apostles would need more time to discuss than we can give. Again and again the original evil state of things at Corinth is touched on, and then always there is a return to the setting forth of the right spirit which would make such scandals impossible. In these later chapters there is special insistence on love as, so to speak, the deepest root of the matter, as it had been set forth by St Paul in writing to that same Corinthian Church. The demand which it makes for self-suppression and self-surrender is illustrated by examples both from among God's saints of old and from among heathens who sacrificed themselves for their fellow-citizens. "These things have they done and will do, that live as citizens of that commonwealth of God for belonging to which there is no regret" (54).

As the end of the Epistle draws near, the Romans by the mouth of Clement declare themselves now guiltless of the sin of the Corinthian malcontents, should it be persevered in; and break forth in a prayer equally memorable for its own sake and for the large borrowings from it which are found in various later

Greek liturgies. It begins with asking that we
may hope on Thy Name, &c. "Grant unto us,
Lord, that we may set our hope on Thy Name
which is the primal source of all creation, and
open the eyes of our hearts, that we may know
Thee, who alone 'abidest Highest in the highest,
Holy in the holy ; who layest low the insolence
of the proud, who scatterest the imaginings of
nations ; who settest the lowly on high, and
bringest the lofty low ; who makest rich and
makest poor' ; who 'killest and makest alive' ;
who alone art the Benefactor of spirits and the
God of all flesh ; who 'lookest into the abysses,'
who scannest the works of man ; the Succour of
them that are in peril, the 'Saviour of them
that are in despair' ; the Creator and Overseer
of every spirit ; who multipliest the nations
upon earth, and hast chosen out from all men
those that love Thee through Jesus Christ, Thy
beloved Son, through whom Thou didst instruct
us, didst sanctify us, didst honour us. We
beseech Thee, Lord and Master, to be our help
and succour. Save those among us who are in
tribulation ; have mercy on the lowly ; lift up
the fallen ; shew Thyself unto the needy ; heal
the ungodly ; convert the wanderers of Thy

people; feed the hungry; release our prisoners; raise up the weak, comfort the faint-hearted. Let all the Gentiles know that 'Thou art God alone' and Jesus Christ is Thy Son and 'we are Thy people and the sheep of Thy pasture[1]'." The prayer for the Christian community presently expands into universality (" Give concord and peace both to us and to all that inhabit the earth"); and then, in the true spirit of St Paul and St Peter, specially makes supplication for the rulers of the Roman empire, " Thou through Thine operations didst make manifest the everlasting fabric of the world. Thou, Lord, didst create the earth. Thou that art faithful throughout all generations, righteous in Thy judgments, marvellous in strength and excellence, Thou that art wise in creating and prudent in establishing that which Thou hast made, that art good in the things which are seen and faithful with them that trust on Thee, pitiful and compassionate, forgive us our iniquities and our unrighteousness and our transgressions and shortcomings. Lay not to our account every sin of Thy servants and Thine handmaids, but cleanse us with the cleansing of Thy truth, and

[1] Lightfoot, *Clement of Rome*, Appendix, p. 376.

guide our steps to walk in holiness and righteousness and singleness of heart and to do such
things as are good and well-pleasing in Thy
sight and in the sight of our rulers.   Yea, Lord,
make Thy face to shine upon us in peace for
our good, that we may be sheltered by Thy
mighty hand and delivered from every sin by
Thine uplifted arm.   And deliver us from them
that hate us wrongfully.   Give concord and
peace to us and to all that dwell on the earth,
as Thou gavest to our fathers, when they called
on Thee in faith and truth with holiness, that
we may be saved, while we render obedience to
Thine almighty and most excellent Name, and
to our rulers and governors upon the earth.

"Thou, Lord and Master, hast given them the
power of sovereignty through Thine excellent
and unspeakable might, that we knowing the
glory and honour which Thou hast given them
may submit ourselves unto them, in nothing
resisting Thy will.   Grant unto them therefore,
O Lord, health, peace, concord, stability, that
they may administer the government which
Thou hast given them without failure.   For
Thou, O heavenly Master, King of the ages,
givest to the sons of men glory and honour and

power over all things that are upon the earth. Do Thou, Lord, direct their counsel according to that which is good and well-pleasing in Thy sight, that, administering in peace and gentleness with godliness the power which Thou hast given them, they may obtain Thy favour. O Thou, who alone art able to do these things and things far more exceeding good than these for us, we praise Thee through the High-priest and Guardian of our souls, Jesus Christ, through whom be the glory and the majesty unto Thee both now and for all generations and for ever and ever. Amen[1]."

The Epistle closes with a few more quiet sentences on its principal theme, and with the commendation of two members of the Roman Church sent as bearers of the letter, " faithful and prudent men, that from youth to old age have walked blamelessly among us, who shall also be witnesses between you and us."

The unaffected loftiness of this Epistle of Clement of Rome, and its position at the head of post-biblical Christian literature, have been a temptation to give it a somewhat disproportionate amount of time. What is called the second

---

[1] Lightfoot, *Clement of Rome*, Appendix, pp. 377 foll.

Epistle of Clement, really an anonymous homily,
a generation or two later in date, may be left
alone, though important for the history of
doctrine. It is rather eccentric in character,
though less so than the early Epistle which
bears the name of Barnabas. Whoever may be
the author of that Epistle, he was certainly not
the Barnabas of the New Testament; and
though full of points of interest to advanced
students, the Epistle is one which for our purpose may be passed over with little loss.

After Clement of Rome we come to Hermas
of Rome. We need not trouble ourselves about
his precise date, which is much disputed. At
earliest he was a contemporary of Clement, at
latest half a century later. He was a brother,
possibly an elder brother, of Pius, who was
bishop of Rome about the middle of the second
century. He was evidently a layman, apparently
engaged in commercial pursuits. By birth,
according to his first words, he was a slave.
His book, which from an early time was called
The Shepherd, was read in various churches in
the first centuries ; and the Latin translation,
which till lately was the only form known of it,
had a certain popularity in Western Europe in

the Middle Ages, so that it is even found in or
after the Old Testament in several manuscripts
of the Latin Bible.   It has often been compared
to the Pilgrim's Progress, and with good reason.
It contains in an imaginative form the thoughts
and broodings of a simple-minded devout man,
on whom the evil that he feels within him and
sees around him lies as a heavy burden, more
especially the evil which he cannot help recognising within the Church itself, the holy society
of God's own chosen people.   'Repentance' is
perhaps the idea that he cherishes most.   He is
entirely free from bitterness or arrogance ; and
the messages which he delivers he delivers not
as from himself but as entrusted to him by one
or other kind of Divine messenger.

The first part of the book consists of five
Visions.   In the first he receives a rebuke for a
sinful thought of his own ; and then presently
for his tolerating the misdeeds of his children,
which had brought loss upon him.   The speaker
in the latter part of this vision is an aged lady
in bright apparel, sitting on a seat of snow-
white wool ; who in the second vision is revealed
to him to be not, as he supposed, the Sibyl, but
the Church.   The third vision, a very striking

one, is chiefly of a tower in process of building upon the waters, made of squared shining stones, i.e. again the Church, built of men (living stones, as St Peter would say) who fit rightly into their place, other stones being partially or wholly cast away. In the fourth vision a great monster from whose mouth proceed fiery locusts is seen and interpreted to be the great tribulation, which is approaching to try the faint-hearted and double-minded that they may be purified for God's use. The fifth vision in a manner includes the rest (above three-fourths) of the book. It begins thus: "When I had been praying in my house, and had seated myself on the bed, there came in a certain man of glorious appearance, in the guise of a shepherd, clothed in a white (goat's) skin, and having a wallet on his shoulders and a staff in his hand. And he greeted me, and I returned his greeting. And straightway he sat down beside me and saith to me, 'I have been sent by the angel of highest dignity, that I may dwell with thee the remaining days of thy life'." The shepherd presently bids him write down the commandments and the parables which he would declare to him. He is then described as the Shepherd, the angel of repentance.

Thenceforth he reappears several times, almost to the end of the book.

Then come twelve Commandments, as they are called. The first is a short one, " First of all believe that God is One, He who created and frames all things, and made all things out of what is not, [bringing them] into being, and containeth all things, but alone is uncontained. Trust Him therefore and fear Him, and fearing practise self-restraint. Keep these things, and thou shalt cast from thyself all wickedness, and put on every virtue of righteousness, and shalt live to God, if thou keepest this commandment." The subjects of the other commandments are truthfulness, chastity, long-suffering, the ways and the angels of good and of evil, right and wrong fear, right and wrong abstinence, the need of faith for prayer, the evil of a gloomy spirit, the true and the false prophet, good and evil desire.

After the twelve Commandments come ten (or more strictly nine) Parables or Similitudes. They are almost wholly taken from country scenes and agricultural or pastoral occupations, specially from vines and other trees. Perhaps the most interesting is the eighth. The angel

shews Hermas "a great willow-tree, overshadow-
ing plains and mountains, and under the shade
of the willow had come all that have been called
by the Name of the Lord." This mighty tree
which overshadowed plains and mountains and
all the earth, is explained to be the Law of God
which was given "to go forth into all the world:
and this law is the Son of God proclaimed unto
the ends of the earth; and the peoples that are
under the shade are they that heard the pro-
clamation and believed on Him." These last
words refer to the next incident of the parable:
"There stood an angel of the Lord glorious
exceedingly, in height above the willow tree,
holding a great reaping-hook, and he cut down
branch after branch from the willow, and gave
to the people that were overshadowed by the
willow.......And after that all had received their
twigs, the angel laid aside his reaping-hook, and
the tree was sound just as I had seen it before."
Presently the angel asks back the twigs, and
receives them one by one, some withered and
gnawed as by a moth, others withered only,
others half withered, others half withered and
cracked, and so on in various gradations to
those which were wholly green and clothed with

fresh shoots and fruit. Those who had held these last were crowned with palm-leaves. This is perhaps the most remarkable example of the just and truthful habit of mind which leads Hermas in various places to mark the various gradations in which good and evil are actually mixed in the hearts and lives of men. The Shepherd invites Hermas to join in planting the other twigs, which in various degrees had lost their greenness, if perchance some of them might live when they have been duly watered: for, said the Shepherd, "He that created this tree willeth that all should live who have received branches from this tree."

With these words we may part company from Hermas.

LECTURE II.

IGNATIUS AND POLYCARP.

LAST week we had for our subject the two
earliest Christian Fathers belonging to the
Roman Church, Clement of Rome the writer of
the Epistle sent by the Church of Rome to the
Church of Corinth, and Hermas the writer of
the book of Visions, Commandments, and
Parables which takes the name '*The Shepherd*'
from the prominent part played in it by the
Angel of Repentance, who appeared to Hermas
in the guise of a shepherd. To-day we proceed
to the others of the Fathers commonly called
Apostolic, who have special claims to be remembered. These are Ignatius of Antioch and
Polycarp of Smyrna.

The names of these cities remind us at once
that we are passing into very different worlds
from that world which immediately surrounded

Clement and Hermas ; and one at least of the
two Eastern Fathers, Ignatius, is singularly
unlike his two brethren of the West.   Ignatius
was Bishop of the Christian Church at Antioch.
Beyond this bare fact we know nothing of his
life and work before the last journey to which
his letters belong.   We can see from the letters
that he had been condemned to death as a
Christian at Antioch and sent off under a guard
of ten soldiers to suffer death at Rome.   The
course taken was, in part at least, through Asia
Minor and then through Macedonia.   Arrived
at Smyrna, he was welcomed not only by the
church of the city and its bishop Polycarp, but
also by the delegates of the churches of three
other cities lying along what we should now call
the loop line of road which he had not traversed,
and especially the church of the great capital,
Ephesus.   During this short stay at Smyrna he
wrote three letters (which have been preserved)
to these three churches which he had been
obliged to pass unvisited, and a fourth of a
different character to the Church of Rome, the
goal of his journey, the place where he expected
and desired to suffer martyrdom.   We next find
him   at Alexandria Troas, the seaport from

which he was to sail for Europe. There he had
the happiness of being overtaken by two deacons
from the neighbourhood of his own Antioch,
and receiving news of the cessation of the
persecution which had caused his own condemnation. There also he wrote three more letters,
to the Church of Smyrna which he had just left,
to Polycarp its bishop, and to the Church of
Philadelphia which he had been allowed to visit
on his way to Smyrna. Thus the seven letters
are made up, which are now in our hands. Of
the European part of his course we have traces
in Polycarp's Epistle, to which we shall come
just now. The Church of Philippi received him
warmly, and at his request sent a letter of
greeting to the Church of Antioch through
Polycarp, as he had asked those other churches
to do to which he had written after receiving
the good tidings from Syria. The Philippian
Christians at the same time took the opportunity
to ask Polycarp for copies of any letters of
Ignatius in his possession. Of what followed
we know nothing beyond the bare fact that
Ignatius suffered martyrdom at Rome. Two
different narratives exist professing to describe
his martyrdom : but they are fabrications of late

date. It is morally certain that the manner of
death would be by the fangs of wild beasts, and
that the place of it would be the vast Flavian
amphitheatre which for many centuries has been
called the Colosseum. Any one who may have
the good fortune to visit Rome and stand within
the ruins of that wonderful pile will do well to
think of Ignatius, and the testimony which he
bore. The time of Ignatius' martyrdom is
known on less clear evidence than could be
wished. The probabilities however are in favour
of about A.D. 110, the time fixed by Lightfoot
in general terms.

We must now turn to the substance of the
letters themselves. It is impossible not to
shrink in some degree from any attempt to
analyse them, as almost a cold-blooded thing to
do. Nothing in early Christian literature is at
all like them ; nothing else has the same in-
tensely personal character. It may be that
their peculiarity is in part owing to difference of
race : we seem to hear a Syrian speaking to us,
not a Greek, much less a Roman, though Ignatius is a Roman name. But a strong personal
individuality is there too. Utterly unlike as
they likewise are in other ways to all the

apostolic Epistles, they have here and there a certain affinity of spirit to the Second Epistle to the Corinthians, the most individual of all St Paul's Epistles. The thought that underlies every word is the thought that the writer is a man sentenced to death, to death for the name of his Lord. The thought brings with it a sense of keen and yet utterly humble exultation. As he passes through the cities of Asia, his constant impulse is towards close fellowship between himself and the various churches in their midst, and again between these and his own church of Antioch. By word and by letter he is constantly striving to make them sharers in his own fervour of martyrdom, and to make himself a sharer in all that concerned their welfare.

Here and there we find warnings against doctrinal errors to the influence of which these Asiatic churches were exposed, apparently of two types only ; one, the early form of what is commonly called Docetism, the tendency so to dwell on our Lord's Divine nature as to regard His body as a mere unreal appearance ; the other the subordination of the Christian faith to Judaism, somewhat as in the days of St Paul. This latter evil was specially rife at Philadelphia,

where the Judaizers seem to have raised oppo-
sition against Ignatius himself as he passed
through.

But a larger part of the letters is taken up
with practical exhortations, especially to unity
of spirit, unity of worship, unity of organisation.
Even at this early time the churches evidently
had many members who had become careless
about Christian fellowship, and neglectful of the
means by which alone it could be preserved in
warmth and vigour.   To take one significant
example, it would seem that many of the
Asiatic Christians had got into a habit of
celebrating the Holy Communion in a loose
and haphazard way, meeting together in little
private knots of people, rather than in the
central congregation as members of one great
body. In this as in all matters Ignatius endeavoured to revive and strengthen internal and
external fellowship by exhorting the members
of the Church to gather dutifully round its duly
appointed officers who were organised in a com-
pact body of three orders, the bishop at the
head, the presbytery or college of elders who
formed his council, and the deacons or servants
(διάκονοι) who were chiefly occupied in the

arrangements for the relief of the poorer members of the Church. Ignatius' language on
these subjects, sometimes startling enough at
best, becomes at least more intelligible when
this practical purpose of his is remembered[1].
Having a keen sense of the immediate evil, he
eagerly has recourse to that external remedy
which lay immediately ready to his hand.

But it is poor work attempting to describe
the words of a man like Ignatius. A few
extracts will give a truer impression of him.
We will begin with one of the elaborate salu-
tations which head his letters, that to the
Philadelphians.

"Ignatius, who is also Theophorus, to the
church of God the Father and of Jesus Christ,
which is in Philadelphia of Asia, which hath
found mercy and is firmly established in the
concord of God and rejoiceth in the passion of
our Lord and in His resurrection without
wavering, being fully assured in all mercy ;
which church I salute in the blood of Jesus
Christ, that is eternal and abiding joy ; more
especially if they be at one with the bishop and
the presbyters who are with him, and with the

[1] See Lightfoot, *Philippians*, pp. 234 foll. and elsewhere.

deacons that have been appointed according to
the mind of Jesus Christ, whom after His own
will He confirmed and established by His Holy
Spirit[1]."

Writing to the Ephesians he says,

"I know who I am and to whom I write.
I am a convict, ye have received mercy: I am
in peril, ye are established. Ye are the high-
road of those that are on their way to die unto
God. Ye are associates in the mysteries with
Paul, who was sanctified, who obtained a good
report, who is worthy of all felicitation; in whose
footsteps I would fain be found treading, when
I shall attain unto God; who in every letter
maketh mention of you in Christ Jesus.

"Do your diligence therefore to meet together
more frequently for thanksgiving to God and
for His glory. For when ye meet together
frequently, the powers of Satan are cast down;
and his mischief cometh to nought in the concord of your faith. There is nothing better
than peace, in which all warfare of things in
heaven and things on earth is abolished.

"None of these things is hidden from you, if

[1] Lightfoot, *Apostolic Fathers*, Part II., Vol. II., Sect. i.,
p. 559.

ye be perfect in your faith and love toward
Jesus Christ, for these are the beginning and
end of life—faith is the beginning and love is
the end—and the two being found in unity are
God, while all things else follow in their train
unto true nobility. No man professing faith
sinneth, and no man possessing love hateth.
'The tree is manifest from its fruit'; so they
that profess to be Christ's shall be seen through
their actions. For the Work is not a thing of
profession now, but is seen then when one is
found in the power of faith unto the end.

"It is better to keep silence and to be, than
to talk and not to be. It is a fine thing to
teach, if the speaker practise. Now there is one
teacher, who 'spake and it came to pass': yea
and even the things which He spake in silence
are worthy of the Father. He that truly pos-
sesseth the word of Jesus, is able also to hearken
unto His silence, that he may be perfect; that
through his speech he may act and through his
silence he may be known."[1]

And again a little earlier,

"And pray ye also without ceasing for the

---

[1] Lightfoot, *Apostolic Fathers*, Part II., Vol. II., Sect. i.,
p. 543.

rest of mankind (for there is in them a hope of repentance) that they may find God.   Therefore permit them to take lessons at least from your works.   Against their outbursts of wrath be ye meek ; against their proud words be ye humble ; against their railings set ye your prayers ; against their errors be ye steadfast in the faith ; against their fierceness be ye gentle.   And be not zealous to imitate them by requital.   Let us shew ourselves their brothers by our forbearance ; but let us be zealous to be imitators of the Lord, vying with each other who shall suffer the greater wrong, who shall be defrauded, who shall be set at nought ; that no herb of the devil be found in you : but in all purity and temperance abide ye in Christ Jesus, with your flesh and with your spirit."[1]

For a comprehensive passage on unity we may take this from the Epistle to the Magnesians.

"Seeing then that in the aforementioned persons I beheld your whole people in faith and embraced them, I advise you, be ye zealous to do all things in godly concord, the bishop

---

[1] Lightfoot, *Apostolic Fathers*, Part II., Vol. II., Sect. i., p. 542.

presiding after the likeness of God and the presbyters after the likeness of the council of the Apostles, with the deacons also who are most dear to me, having been entrusted with the diaconate of Jesus Christ, who was with the Father before the worlds and appeared at the end of time. Therefore do ye all study conformity to God and pay reverence one to another ; and let no man regard his neighbour after the flesh, but love ye one another in Christ Jesus always. Let there be nothing among you which shall have power to divide you, but be ye united with the bishop and with them that preside over you as an ensample and a lesson of incorruptibility.

"Therefore as the Lord did nothing without the Father, [being united with Him], either by Himself or by the Apostles, so neither do ye anything without the bishop and the presbyters. And attempt not to think anything right for yourselves apart from others ; but let there be one prayer in common, one supplication, one mind, one hope, in love and in joy unblameable, which is Jesus Christ, than whom there is nothing better. Hasten to come together all of you, as to one temple, even God ; as to one altar, even

to one Jesus Christ, who came forth from One
Father and is with One and departed unto One."[1]

These passages are from letters to churches,
the six Asiatic churches to which he wrote.
We may take also a few words from the beginning of his one letter to a single man, Polycarp the Bishop of Smyrna.

"Ignatius who is also Theophorus, unto
Polycarp, who is bishop of the Church of
the Smyrnæans, or rather whose Bishop is
God the Father and Jesus Christ, abundant
greeting.

"Welcoming thy godly mind which is
grounded as it were on an immovable rock,
I give exceeding glory that it hath been vouchsafed me to see thy blameless face, whereof I
would fain have joy in God. I exhort thee in
the grace wherewith thou art clothed to press forward in thy course and to exhort all men that
they may be saved. Vindicate thine office in all
diligence of flesh and of spirit. Have a care for
union, than which there is nothing better. Bear
all men, as the Lord also beareth thee. Suffer
all men in love, as also thou doest. Give thyself

[1] Lightfoot, *Apostolic Fathers*, Part II., Vol. II., Sect. i.,
p. 547.

to unceasing prayers. Ask for larger wisdom
than thou hast. Be watchful, and keep thy
spirit from slumbering. Speak to each man
severally after the manner of God. Bear the
maladies of all, as a perfect athlete. Where
there is much toil, there is much gain."[1]

I have kept till last the Epistle to the
Romans, which is of different character from
the rest. This was the church which was to receive
him last; at Rome he was to die. To the Roman
Christians he pours forth his inmost thoughts
about his martyrdom. The exhortation which
he has to address to them is chiefly that they
will do nothing to hinder him in attaining this
object of his desire. It is probable enough that
among them were to be found persons of much
influence with the emperor, who might thus have
been able to save his life. But this is what he
most anxiously deprecates. It must be confessed
that much of the language here used about
martyrdom is out of harmony with the teaching
of the Lord and His Apostles. Taken up by
men of a lower type of mind and character, it
led but too naturally to the mere frensy of self-

[1] Lightfoot, *Apostolic Fathers*, Part II., Vol. II., Sect. i.,
p. 567.

destruction, under the name of martyrdom,
against which some of the wiser Fathers had
afterwards to protest. But reverence is due
even to the extravagances of such a lofty soul
as that of Ignatius.

"Ignatius, who is also Theophorus, unto her
that hath found mercy in the bountifulness of the
Father Most High and of Jesus Christ His only
Son ; to the Church that is beloved and enlight-
ened through the will of Him who willed all
things that are, by faith and love towards Jesus
Christ our God ; even unto her that hath the
presidency in the country of the region of the
Romans, being worthy of God, worthy of honour,
worthy of felicitation, worthy of praise, worthy
of success, worthy in purity, and having the
presidency of love, walking in the law of Christ
and bearing the Father's name; which Church
also I salute in the name of Jesus Christ the Son
of the Father; unto them that in flesh and spirit
are united unto His every commandment, being
filled with the grace of God without wavering,
and filtered clear from every foreign stain; abundant greeting in Jesus Christ our God in blame-
lessness.

"Forasmuch as in answer to my prayer to

God it hath been granted to me to see your godly countenances, ·so that I have obtained even more than I asked; for wearing bonds in Christ Jesus I hope to salute you, if it be the Divine will that I should be counted worthy to reach unto the end; for the beginning verily is well ordered, if so be I shall attain unto the goal, that I may receive mine inheritance without hindrance. For I dread your very love, lest it do me an injury: for it is easy for you to do what ye will, but for me it is difficult to attain unto God, unless ye shall spare me.

"For I would not have you to be men pleasers but to please God, as indeed ye do please Him. For neither shall I myself ever find an opportunity such as this to attain unto God, nor can ye, if ye be silent, win the credit of any nobler work. For if ye be silent and leave me alone, I am a word of God; but if ye desire my flesh, then shall I be again a mere cry. Nay grant me nothing more than that I be poured out a libation to God, while there is still an altar ready; that forming yourselves into a chorus in love ye may sing to the Father in Jesus Christ, for that God hath vouchsafed that the bishop from Syria should be found in the West, having summoned him from the East. It is good to set from the world unto God, that I may rise unto Him."

"I write to all the churches, and I bid all men know, that of my own free will I die for God, unless ye should hinder me. Let me be given to the wild beasts, for through them I can attain unto God. I am God's wheat, and I am ground by the teeth of wild beasts that I may be found pure bread [of Christ]. Rather entice the wild beasts, that they may become my sepulchre and may leave no part of my body behind, so that I may not, when I am fallen asleep, be burdensome to anyone. Then shall I be truly a disciple of Jesus Christ, when the world shall not so much as see my body. Supplicate the Lord for me, that through these instruments I may be found a sacrifice to God. I do not enjoin you, as Peter and Paul did. They were apostles, I am a convict; they were free, but I am a slave this very hour. Yet if I shall suffer, then am I a freedman of Jesus Christ, and I shall rise free in Him. Now I am learning in my bonds to put away every desire.

"Remember in your prayers the church which is in Syria, which hath God for its shepherd in my stead. Jesus Christ alone shall be

its bishop. He and your love. But for myself
I am ashamed to be called one of them; for
neither am I worthy, being the very last of them
and an untimely birth : but I have found mercy
that I should be some one, if so be I shall attain
unto God. My spirit saluteth you, and the love
of the churches which received me in the name
of Jesus Christ, not as a mere wayfarer; for even
those churches which did not lie on my route
after the flesh went before me from city to city.

"Now I write these things unto you from
Smyrna by the hand of the Ephesians who are
worthy of all felicitation. And Crocus also, a
name very dear to me, is with me, with many
others besides."[1]

Polycarp, we have seen, was the chief person.
with whom Ignatius was brought in contact on
his journey as a condemned prisoner through
Asia Minor. There are other proper names in
tolerable abundance in the Ignatian letters: but
they belong to men now forgotten, and even in
that day none of them can have had the pro-
minence of Polycarp. His own one extant
writing belongs to this very time : i.e. it was

[1] Lightfoot, *Apostolic Fathers*, Part II., Vol. II., Sect. i.,
pp. 555, foll.

written after Ignatius had not only left Asia
Minor but Philippi also, but when as yet no
tidings had come from Italy as to what had
befallen him at Rome. This writing is a letter
to the Philippians in answer to that which they
had written on Ignatius' departure. To it were
appended copies of the letters written by Ignatius
to Smyrna and other churches, and these copies
are probably the source of our present collection.

The letter itself has no such vivid personal
interest as those of Ignatius. The good Polycarp was a much more commonplace person.
But apart from its connexion with Ignatius, his
letter has a great value of its own, partly as
shewing what manner of thoughts on Christian
faith and practice the bishop of a great Asiatic
city cherished at that early date, partly also as
shewing what writings of the Apostles he
possessed and revered and drew upon (and that
copiously) to give point and authority to what
he had to say. The letter is for the most part
made up of brotherly admonition, partly to
the Philippian church at large, partly to its
deacons, partly to its elders. There is no
mention of any bishop, any more than there is in
Ignatius' epistle to the Romans. Apparently this

concentration of church government had not yet
at this time spread from Asia into Europe. We
may take a short chapter from near the beginning (after the Salutation), and another from near
the end.

"I rejoiced with you greatly in our Lord
Jesus Christ, for that ye received the followers
of the true love and escorted them on their way,
as befitted you—those men encircled in saintly
bonds which are the diadems of them that
be truly chosen of God and our Lord; and
that the stedfast root of your faith which was
famed from primitive times abideth until now
and beareth fruit unto our Lord Jesus Christ,
who endured to face even death for our sins,
'whom God raised, having loosed the pangs
of Hades; on whom, though ye saw Him not,
ye believe with joy unutterable and full of
glory'; unto which joy many desire to enter
in; forasmuch as ye know that it is 'by grace
ye are saved, not of works,' but by the will
of God through Jesus Christ."[1]

"For I am persuaded that ye are well
trained in the sacred writings, and nothing

---

[1] Lightfoot, *Apostolic Fathers*, Part II., Vol. II., Sect. ii.,
p. 1051.

is hidden from you. But to myself this is
not granted. Only, as it is said in the scriptures,
'Be ye angry and sin not' and 'Let not the
sun set on your wrath.' Blessed is he that
remembereth this; and I trust that this is in
you. Now may the God and Father of our
Lord Jesus Christ, and the eternal High Priest
Himself, the God Jesus Christ, build you up
in faith and truth, and in all gentleness and in
all avoidance of wrath and in forbearance and
long suffering and in patient endurance and
purity; and may He grant unto you a lot and
portion among His saints, and to us with you,
and to all that are under heaven, who shall
believe on our Lord and God Jesus Christ
and on His Father 'that raised Him from the
dead. Pray for all the saints.' Pray also
'for kings and powers and princes,' and 'for
them that persecute' and hate 'you,' and for
'the enemies of the cross,' that your fruit may
be 'manifest among all men,' that ye may be
perfect in Him."[1]

This meeting with Ignatius must have come
somewhere towards the middle of Polycarp's

[1] Lightfoot, *Apostolic Fathers*, Part II., Vol. II., Sect. ii.,
p. 1055.

long life. His importance for us depends in
no small degree on that longevity of his. As
Dr Lightfoot has expounded with peculiar
force, he bridges the long and comparatively
obscure period between the close of the apostolic
age and the great writers of the latter part
of the second century. Born somewhere about
the time of the destruction of Jerusalem by
Titus, he lived in early life near St John and
it may be one or two more of the Twelve.
Of this converse in early youth he used to
rejoice to tell in his later years. This we
learn from a striking passage from a letter
of Irenæus which has happily been preserved.
" I can tell" he wrote, "the very place in which
the blessed Paul used to sit when he discoursed,
and his goings out and his comings in, and the
stamp of his life, and his bodily appearance,
and the discourses which he held towards the
congregation, and how he would describe his
intercourse with John and with the rest of those
who had seen the Lord, and how he would
relate their words. And whatsoever things he
had heard from them about the Lord and
about His acts of power and about His teaching,
Polycarp, as having received them from eye-

witnesses of the life and Word would relate
altogether in accordance with the Scriptures."[1]

But from that midpoint of Polycarp's life
formed by the passing of Ignatius we are able
not only to look back to his youth but also
forward to his extreme old age. Somewhere
about the middle of the second century he made
a journey to Rome to take counsel with
Anicetus the Bishop (for by that time episcopacy
was regularly established at Rome) about
various matters of Church usage, but especially
about the time of celebrating the Paschal
festival, as to which the Churches of Asia Minor
differed from those of the West. They remained
in perfect amity, though the differences of usage
continued, and Anicetus paid Polycarp the
honour of setting him in his own place to
preside over the Eucharistic service at Rome.
Not long after the old man's return, something
like forty-five years after Ignatius' death for
conscience sake, he too in his turn was called
to give his life in bearing witness to the truth.
A probably genuine narrative of his martyrdom
still survives, being a letter from the Church
of Smyrna to one or more Churches in Phrygia.

---

[1] Lightfoot, i. 429.   Eusebius, v. 20.

Every one, I suppose, has somewhere or other
read the answer which he is recorded to have
made when the magistrate, anxious to spare
him, besought him to revile the Christ, and
so obtain release. "Fourscore and six years
have I been his servant; and how can I blas-
pheme my King that saved me?" Let us read
also his last words when he had been tied to the
stake, true last words of a true Father of the
Church.

"So they did not nail him, but tied him.
Then he, placing his hands behind him, and
being bound to the stake, like a noble ram out
of a great flock for an offering, a burnt sacrifice
made ready and acceptable to God, looking up
to heaven said; 'O Lord God Almighty, the
Father of Thy beloved and blessed Son Jesus
Christ, through whom we have received the
knowledge of Thee, the God of angels and
powers and of all creation and of the whole race
of the righteous, who live in Thy presence;
I bless Thee for that Thou hast granted me
this day and hour, that I might receive a
portion amongst the number of martyrs in the
cup of [Thy] Christ unto resurrection of eternal
life, both of soul and body, in the incorrupti-

bility of the Holy Spirit. May I be received among these in Thy presence this day, as a rich and acceptable sacrifice, as Thou didst prepare and reveal it beforehand, and hast accomplished it, Thou that art the faithful and true God. For this cause, yea and for all things, I praise Thee, I bless Thee, I glorify Thee, through the eternal and heavenly High-priest, Thy beloved Son, through whom with Him and the Holy Spirit be glory both now [and ever] and for the ages to come. Amen.'"[1]

[1] Lightfoot, *Apostolic Fathers*, Part II., Vol. II., Sect. ii., p. 1064.

LECTURE III.

JUSTIN AND IRENÆUS.

LAST week we finished those of the Fathers who are called Apostolic Fathers. We considered two of them who were also martyrs, though at a long interval of time, one a Bishop of Antioch who was conducted through Asia Minor to perish by the fangs of wild beasts at Rome, the other a Bishop of Smyrna who welcomed him on his way to death, collected his letters and wrote about him at the time, journeyed himself in extreme old age from Asia Minor to Rome to confer about difference of Church usages, came peacefully home, and then before long was himself called to perish at the stake in his own Smyrna because he too would not deny his Lord.

We come to-day to a third martyr, one who conventionally bears the title of martyr almost

as if it were part of his name. Justin was born
at Flavia Neapolis close to Sychem in Samaria,
but, it would seem, of heathen parentage. His
Dialogue, to which we shall come presently, is
represented as having had its scene laid at
Ephesus. Eventually Justin would seem to
have been much at Rome, at that time a special
place of resort for those who took an active part
in religious movements: and there he suffered
martyrdom.

The genuine works of his which have come
down to us in their original form are at most
three in number, without counting a little
treatise against heresies, lost in its original form,
but apparently in great part copied by Irenæus.
Several others bear his name in manuscripts,
but are certainly by other authors of various
ages, some quite late. Early in the fourth
century his name was attached to a partially
different list of writings, the genuineness of
which we have no means of testing. But the
books of his which we do possess are so valuable
from several points of view that we have every
reason to be satisfied. They are two Apologies,
as they are called, defending Christians against
heathen misrepresentations and heathen perse-

cutions; and a Dialogue with a Jew named
Trypho in which the faith of Christians is
vindicated against Judaism. It is hardly necessary to say that Justin's Apologies have nothing
whatever to do with courteous excuses, i.e. with
the modern English sense of the word 'apology.'
It is simply the common Greek word to denote
any kind of defence against any kind of accusa-
tion, in a court of justice or anywhere else.
Justin's Apologies were not quite the earliest of
which we have any knowledge; but, so far as
we do know, their predecessors were of less
permanent value.

Justin's first and longest Apology is addressed
to the Roman Emperor, i.e. Antoninus Pius, and
his two adopted sons, one of them the philosopher Marcus Aurelius, to the Sacred Senate and
all the people of the Romans. The time is
two or three years before the middle of the
second century. Justin writes, he says, on
behalf of them who out of every race of mankind
are the subjects of unjust hate and contumely,
being himself one of them. He begins by ap-
pealing to the names *Pious* and *Philosopher*
borne by the rulers. "Reason," he says, "instructs those who are truly Pious and Philo-

sophers to honour and cherish that only which
is true, refusing to follow mere opinions of the
ancients if they are bad ones: for sober reason
instructs us not only not to follow those actions
or decisions which have been unjust, but the
lover of truth is bound in every way, and with
disregard of his own life, to choose to say and
do such things as are just, though he be
threatened with death for so doing." He pro-
tests against condemnation of Christians for
the mere name, without anything evil being
proved against them. He repudiates the vulgar
imputation of atheism, pointing out how the
same charge had been brought against Socrates,
and had caused his death. That crime he at-
tributes to the inspiration of the demons, whom
he identifies with the gods of the heathen, and
whom he represents as similarly inspiring the
attacks upon Christians. As regards such gods
as these, he confesses atheism, but not as regards the most true God, the Father of right,
and temperance and the other virtues, Himself
free from all mixture of evil; and His Son and
the prophetic Spirit. As regards the lives of
Christians, he courts the fullest enquiry, de-
manding that any found guilty of misconduct

be duly punished, but for his crimes, not for
being a Christian. Then follow several chapters
on the true service of God, on the Divine
kingdom for which Christians look, and on their
living as ever in God's sight; and this is followed
by free quotation from the Sermon on the
Mount, and other similar passages from Gospel
records; and by reference to Christ's own
authority for the faithful loyalty which Christians
practised towards the emperors. But it would
take far too long to give even a slight sketch of
the contents of the Apology. At every step
we find attempts to trace analogies between
Christian beliefs on the one hand and Greek
philosophy or Greek mythology on the other.
This was no mere diplomatic *ad hominem* ac-
commodation, but connected with Justin's own
deepest convictions. The doctrine of the
Divine Word or λόγος received from Scripture he
connected with the Stoic doctrine of the Word or
Reason (λόγος) a seed of which is inborn in all
men ; and thus he was enabled to recognise the
workings of God in the ages before the Word
became Incarnate. He also appeals largely to
the testimony of the Jewish prophets ; but on
this subject he is hampered by his habit of

looking chiefly to supposed literal fulfilments of
verbal predictions and by a want of perception
of the true nature of prophecy. The last few
chapters contain a valuable account of baptism
as then practised (i.e. adult baptism, for nothing
is said of infant baptism), and then of the
conducting of the newly-baptised person to the
assembly of "the brethren," followed by the
offering up of prayers for him and "for all others
everywhere," and by the joining of all in the
feast of thanksgiving or Eucharist, of which he
gives a further explanation. "And we from
that time forward," he proceeds, "always have
each other in remembrance; and we that are
wealthy give help to all that are in need, and
we are in company with each other always.
And for all that we partake of we bless the
Maker of all things through his Son Jesus
Christ and through the Holy Spirit." Last he
describes the Sunday service including the
Eucharist, and the distribution of the offerings
among orphans and widows, the sick and the
needy, prisoners and sojourners from other
lands.

The second or Shorter Apology is probably a
sort of Appendix to the first. It begins with a

complaint how Urbicus the city prefect (or mayor, as we should say) had condemned three Christians in succession to death, without any crime on their part. Justin declares that he too is expecting a similar fate, perhaps by the false accusations of the Cynic Crescens who went about declaiming against the Christians. In what follows Justin speaks still more explicitly than before of the seed of the Word which had been implanted in the wiser and better heathen, causing them to be persecuted, not Socrates only but Musonius and other Stoics: but they all differed, he explains, from Christ, because what with them was in part only was with Him complete and whole. "Whatsoever things therefore," he says, "have been said well in any men's words belong to us Christians: for we worship and love next to God the Word who cometh forth from the unborn and unutterable God, since for our sakes also He hath become man, that becoming also a partaker of the things that affect us He might also accomplish for us a cure. For all those writers were able to see but dimly through the seed of the Word inborn in them the things that are. For a seed of a thing and imitation of it granted according to capacity is one thing, and quite other is that which graciously gives itself to be imparted and imitated."

The other work of Justin, a much larger one, is the Dialogue with Trypho:

"While I was walking one morning in the walks of the Xystus, a certain man, with others in his company, having met me, said, 'Hail, O philosopher!' And immediately after saying this, he turned round and walked along with me; his friends likewise turned round with him. And I for my part addressed him, saying, 'Well, what is it?' And he replied, 'I was taught,' says he, 'by Corinthus the Socratic in Argos, that I ought not to despise or neglect those who wear this dress, but to shew them all kindness, and to associate with them, if so be some advantage might arise from the intercourse either to some such man or to myself. It is good, moreover, for both, if either the one or the other be benefited. On this account, therefore, whenever I see anyone in such dress, I gladly approach him, and now, for the same reason, have I willingly accosted you; and these accompany me, in the expectation of hearing for themselves something profitable from you.'

'But who are you, best of mortals?' So I replied to him in jest.

Then he told me simply both his name and his race. 'Trypho,' says he, 'I am called; and I am a Hebrew of the circumcision, escaped from the war lately carried on there, and now spending my days in Greece, for the most part at Corinth.'

'And in what' said I, 'would you be profited by philosophers so much as by your own lawgiver and the prophets?'

'What?' he replied. 'Do not the philosophers make their whole discourse on God? and are they not continually raising questions about His unity and providence? Is not this truly the duty of philosophy, to investigate concerning the Divinity?'

'Yes,' said I, 'so we too have supposed. But the most have not even cared about this, whether there be one or more gods, and whether they take thought for each one of us or no, as if this knowledge contributed nothing to our happiness; nay, they moreover attempt to persuade us that God takes care of the universe as a whole with its genera and species, but not of me and you, and each individually, since other-

wise we would surely not need to pray to Him
night and day.   But it is not difficult to understand the upshot of this; for fearlessness and
licence in speaking result to such as maintain
these opinions, doing and saying whatever they
choose, neither dreading punishment nor hoping
for any benefit from God.   For how could they?
They affirm that the same things shall always
happen; and, further, that I and you shall again
live in like manner, having become neither
better men nor worse.   But there are some
others, who, having supposed the soul to be
immortal and immaterial, believe that though
they have committed evil they will not suffer
punishment (for that which is immaterial is
insensible), and that the soul, in consequence of
its immortality, needs nothing from God.'

And he, smiling gently, said, 'Tell us your
opinion of these matters, and what idea you
entertain respecting God, and what your philosophy is.'

'I will tell you,' said I, 'what seems to me;
for philosophy is in fact the greatest possession,
and most honourable before God, to whom it
leads us and alone commends us; and these
are truly holy men who have bestowed atten-

tion on philosophy. What philosophy is, however, and the reason why it has been sent down
to men, have escaped the observation of most;
for there would be neither Platonists, nor Stoics,
nor Peripatetics, nor Theoretics, nor Pythago-
reans, this knowledge being one.   I wish to tell
you how it has become many-headed. It has
happened that those who first handled it [i.e.
philosophy], and who were therefore esteemed
illustrious men, were succeeded by those who
made no investigations concerning truth, but
only admired the perseverance and self-discipline
of the former, as well as the novelty of the
doctrines; and each thought that to be true
which he learned from his teacher: then, moreover, those latter persons handed down to their
successors such things, and others similar to
them; and this system was called by the name
of him who was styled the father of the doctrine.
Being at first desirous of personally conversing
with one of these men, I surrendered myself to
a certain Stoic; and having spent a considerable time with him, when I had not acquired
any further knowledge of God (for he did not
know himself nor did he say that this was a
necessary part of teaching) I left him, and be-

took myself to another, who was called a
Peripatetic, and as he fancied, shrewd. And
this man, after putting up with me for the first
few days, requested me to fix a fee, in order
that the intercourse might not be unprofitable
to us. Him too for this reason I abandoned,
believing him to be no philosopher at all. But
as my soul was still yearning to hear the
peculiar and choice part of philosophy, I came
to a Pythagorean, very celebrated—a man who
thought much of his own wisdom. And then,
when I had an interview with him, willing to
become his hearer and disciple, he said, "What
then? Are you acquainted with music, astro-
nomy and geometry? Do you expect to perceive any of those things which conduce to a
happy life, if you have not been first informed
on those points which wean the soul from sen-
sible objects, and render it fitted for objects
which appertain to the mind, so that it can
contemplate that which is honourable in its
essence and that which is good in its essence?"
Having commended many of these branches of
learning, and telling me that they were necessary, he dismissed me when I confessed to him
my ignorance. Accordingly I took it rather

impatiently, as was to be expected when I failed in my hope, the more so because I deemed the man had some knowledge ; but reflecting again on the space of time during which I would have to linger over those branches of learning, I was not able to endure longer procrastination. In my perplexity it occurred to me to have an interview with the Platonists likewise, for their fame was great. And so I conversed much with one who had lately settled in our city—a man of intelligence, holding a high position among the Platonists—and I made progress, and gained ever so much increase day by day. And the perception of immaterial things quite overpowered me, and the contemplation of ideas furnished my mind with wings, so that in a little while I supposed that I had become wise ; and such was my stupidity, I expected forthwith to look upon God, for this is the end of Plato's philosophy.

'And while I was thus disposed, when I wished at one time to be filled with great quietness, and to shun the tramp of men, I used to go to a certain field not far from the sea. And when I was near that spot one day, which having reached I purposed to be by myself, a

certain old man, by no means contemptible in
appearance, shewing a meek and grave dis-
position, followed me at a little distance. And
when I turned round to him, having halted, I
fixed my eyes rather keenly on him.'"—

Then Justin recounts how the old man, after
much discourse on philosophy, and especially
that of Plato and Pythagoras, guided him to
the prophets and the Christ of whom they
prophesied.

"'But pray' he concluded 'that before all
things, the gates of light may be opened to thee;
for these things are not perceptible to the eyes
or mind of all, but only of the man to whom
God and His Christ shall give the power to
understand.'

'When he had spoken these and many other
things, which there is no time for mentioning at
present, he went away, bidding me follow them
up; and I saw him no more. But straightway
a fire was kindled in my soul; and a love of the
prophets, and of those men who are friends of
Christ, possessed me; and whilst revolving his
words in my mind, I found this philosophy
alone to be safe and expedient. Thus, then,
and for this reason, I am a philosopher. More-

over, I would wish that all with a resolution
similar to my own would never separate themselves from the words of the Saviour. For they
possess an awe in themselves, and are sufficient
to abash those who turn aside from the path of
rectitude; while the sweetest rest comes to
those who carefully practise them. If then,
thou hast any care for thyself, and seekest after
salvation and puttest thy trust in God, thou
mayest come to know the Christ of God, and
become perfect, and so be happy.'

When I had said this, my beloved friend,
those who were with Trypho laughed; but he,
smiling, says, ' I approve of your other remarks,
and admire the eagerness with which you study
divine things; but it were better for you still to
abide in the philosophy of Plato, or of some
other man, cultivating endurance, self-control,
and moderation, rather than be deceived by
false words, and follow the opinions of men of
no reputation. For if you remain in that mode
of philosophy, and live blamelessly, a hope of a
better destiny were left to you; but when you
have forsaken God, and reposed confidence in
man, what safety still awaits you? If, then,
thou art willing to listen to me (for I have

already considered you a friend), first be cir-
cumcised, then keep as the law hath ordained
the Sabbath, and the feasts, and the new moons
of God ; and, in a word, do all things which
have been written in the law : and then perhaps
thou shalt have mercy from God.   But Christ—
if He has indeed been born, and exists anywhere—is unknown, and does not yet even
recognise Himself, and has no power until Elias
come to anoint Him, and make Him manifest to
all.   But ye, accepting a vain report, invent a
Christ for yourselves, and for His sake are now
inconsiderately perishing.'

    ' I excuse and forgive you, my friend,' I
said ' for you know not what you say, but have
been persuaded by teachers who do not understand the Scriptures; and you speak, like a
diviner, whatever comes into your mind.   But
if you are willing to listen to an account of
Him, how we have not been deceived, and shall
not cease to confess Him—although men's
reproaches be heaped upon us, although the
most terrible tyrant compel us to deny Him,—
I shall prove to you as you stand here that we
have not believed empty fables, or words without any foundation, but words filled with the

Spirit of God, and big with power, and flourish-
ing with grace[1].' "

Some of Trypho's companions depart with
jeers, and then the dialogue begins in earnest.
It ranges over the various points of difference
between Judaism and the Christian faith of that
time, and large masses of the Old Testament
are naturally quoted and discussed. But we
must be content with the autobiographic sketch,
for such it doubtless is, which forms the introduction. Of course we must not expect that
that story of passing from philosopher to philosopher is a *complete* account of the course of
Justin's conversion. In his second Apology he
speaks strongly of the impression made on him
by the virtues of the Christians while he was in
his Platonist stage, and we may be sure that
this impression acted powerfully on him. But
the name which he commonly bore, Justin
philosopher and martyr, was entirely appropriate.
He is the first prominent representative of what
was to be the characteristic of many Fathers of
the Church both Greek and Latin, the construc-
tion of a theology out of the biblical elements of

[1] Justin Martyr, *Dialogue with Trypho*, from pp. 85—97 in
Rev. G. Reith's translation (Antenicene Christian Library).

the faith in combination with this or that
Gentile philosophy of the loftier sort.

How soon Justin's anticipations of martyrdom were fulfilled is not known with certainty.
There is fair evidence however that the interval
was not long. A short and simple narrative of
his examination before the prefect still survives,
and is almost certainly genuine. He and his
companions died by the headsman's sword.

We possess other Greek Apologies written
later in the same century. The most individual
of them is by Tatian, an erratic disciple of
Justin's, the compiler of a famous Diatessaron
or composite Gospel narrative formed by putting
together small fragments of the four Gospels.
He was by birth a Syrian, not a Greek, and his
fiery nature bursts forth in his Apology in bitter
hatred and contempt for all that was Greek.
The other Apologies have a value of their own,
but are far below Justin's in force and freshness.

We must now turn to a different region from
any in which we have as yet paused. Irenæus,
one of the greatest of the Fathers, belongs to
different countries; but he must always be
chiefly associated with South-East France, the
scene of his principal labours and episcopal

authority. There is however a prelude to his
work which must not be passed over. Mar-
seilles was a Greek colony of great antiquity;
and from it the Greek language and culture
spread not only along the coast but for a considerable distance up the Rhone. How the
Gospel first found its way there we do not
know: but there is some evidence of a connexion between the churches of Western Asia
Minor and those of the Rhone. Now the
historian Eusebius has preserved for us the
greater part of a letter which begins thus:

"The servants of Christ who sojourn in
Vienne and Lyons in Gaul to the brethren
throughout Asia and Phrygia who have the
same faith and hope of redemption with us:
peace and grace and glory from God the Father
and Christ Jesus our Lord." The purpose of
the letter is to describe a grievous persecution
which had fallen upon them, Pothinus the
bishop, a man of 90 years of age, being among
the victims. The story of Christian heroism,
especially as shewn by the slave girl Blandina,
has hardly an equal in literature: but it must be
read as a whole, and it is of considerable length.

While some of these Christians of Lyons and

Vienne were in prison, they wrote various letters, among others one to Eleutherus, Bishop of Rome, "on behalf of the peace of the churches," i.e. probably to urge toleration for the votaries of the new enthusiastic movement proceeding from Phrygia which we know under the name Montanism.   The bearer of the letter was an elder of Lyons, Irenæus by name ; and the writers of the letter warmly commend him to Eleutherus, as one who was zealous for the covenant of Christ.   How long he had been in Gaul, we know not ; but he came from Asia Minor, where as we know from the passage read last week he had listened eagerly to the aged Polycarp, and his reminiscences of his intercourse in youth with men who had seen the Lord. There is also some evidence that he was at Rome at the time of Polycarp's death, and heard there the sound as of a trumpet proclaiming "Polycarp hath suffered martyrdom."   Later in life he addressed himself to Rome for another mission of peace.   The importance which the Church of Rome derived from its position in the central city of the Empire was gradually fastening itself to the person of its bishop, and assumed   exaggerated   proportions   when   the

arrogant Victor was its bishop. The differences
between the Asiatic and the Roman customs as
to the time of keeping the Paschal festival had
now become aggravated into a deadly strife,
and Victor endeavoured to impose the Roman
custom on all churches. Irenæus was now a
follower of the Roman custom : but this did not
prevent his writing a strong letter of remonstrance to Victor in the name of the Christians
of Gaul.   This incident occurred somewhere
in the last few years of the second century.
After this we hear no more of Irenæus on any
tolerable authority. He may or may not have
lived into the new century. Essentially he is
the best representative of the last half, and
especially the last quarter, of the second century.

Besides minor works, chiefly Epistles, of
which we have only fragments, we possess
entire Irenæus' great work, the Refutation and
Overthrow of the Knowledge (Gnosis) falsely so
called. Only a small proportion of it is preserved in Greek : but it is a great thing that the
ancient Latin version is completely preserved.
Thus far I have said nothing about the theologians who are now called Gnostics. Unfortu-

nately not many fragments are preserved of
their own writings; so that our knowledge of
them comes chiefly from opponents who saw
truly the impossibility of reconciling their main
principles with the historical Gospel, but who as
a rule had but a dim sense of the real meaning
of their speculations, and a very imperfect
sympathy with the speculative difficulties which
led to them. The so-called Gnostic systems
were various attempts to interpret history and
nature by a medley of Christian ideas with the
ideas and mythologies suggested by various
Eastern religions. The most definite types of so-
called Gnosticism were further shaped by Greek
influence, and it is in this form that they chiefly
came into collision with the ordinary churches.
Their great time was about the middle of the
first half of the second century: but they lasted
on in one shape or another for a considerable
time. The great leaders had passed away
before Irenæus wrote: but even in Gaul his
flock was troubled by some of the successors;
and it was no superfluous task that he under-
took when he set about an elaborate refutation.
Doubtless he had other predecessors besides
Justin. Thus Papias had written " Expositions

of the Lord's Oracles" to correct and supersede
the fantastic interpretation of our Lord's
parables and other discourses by which some
of the so-called Gnostics endeavoured to find
authority for their speculations. Nor was he
the only 'elder,' to use the often recurring title,
whom Irenæus was thankful to quote and sometimes to transcribe at considerable length.
Doubtless, if so large a proportion of the Christian
literature of the preceding half-century had not
perished, we should have found yet clearer evidence of the width of his reading.

But it is a striking fact that, while his censure
of the so-called Gnostic systems is always un-
reserved and pitiless, he is unconsciously influ-
enced by the new thoughts which they had
brought forward. The Christianity which he
proclaims has a comprehensiveness such as no
earlier Christian Father known to us could ever
have dreamed of. His doctrine of the Word is
a true expansion of St John's doctrine, a rich
application of it to bring order into the retro-
spect of the spiritual history of mankind : and
so his vision of the future is inspired by the
thought which he loves to repeat out of the
Epistle to the Ephesians, how that it was the

eternal purpose of the Father to sum up all things in Christ (ἀνακεφαλαιώσασθαι, *recapitulare*).

Two passages must suffice, though many are tempting to read. The first shall be a familiar one from the second book, on our Lord's taking upon Him all the ages of man up to adult manhood.

" He was thirty years of age when He came to the Baptism, thenceforth having the full age of a teacher, when He came to Jerusalem, that He might rightly be able to receive the title of Teacher from all. For to seem one thing, and *be* another, was not His way, as is said by those who represent Him as being in appearance only: but what He was, that He also seemed. Being therefore a Teacher, He had likewise the ages of a Teacher, not rejecting nor transcending man, nor breaking the law of the human race in Himself, but hallowing every age by its likeness to Himself. For He came to save all through Himself; all, I mean, who through Him are born anew unto God, infants, and little children, and boys, and youths, and elders. Accordingly He came through every age, with infants becoming an infant, hallowing infants; among

little children a little child, hallowing those of
that very age, at the same time making Himself
to them an example of dutifulness, and righteousness, and subjection; among young men a
young man, becoming an example to young
men and hallowing them to the Lord. So also
an elder among elders, that He might be a
perfect Teacher in all things, not only as regards
the setting forth of the Truth but also as regards
age, at the same time hallowing also the elders,
becoming likewise an example to them. Lastly
He came also even unto death, that He might
be the first begotten from the dead, Himself
holding the primacy in all things, the Author of
life, before all things, and having precedence of
all things[1]."

The other passage shall be from the end of
the book, the end also of the millennial speculations which filled Irenæus as they did other
men of that age. If some of the thoughts are
difficult to follow, yet they manifestly deserve
to be listened to and pondered.

" In clear vision then did John see beforehand the first resurrection of the righteous, and
the inheritance of the earth during the kingdom

[1] Irenæus, p. 358, Stieren.

(reign) : to the same effect also did the prophets prophesy concerning it. For thus much the Lord also taught, in that He promised that He would have a new mixing of the Cup in the kingdom with the disciples. And the apostle too declared that the creation should be free from the bondage of corruption to enter the liberty of the glory of the sons of God. And in all these [events], and through them all, the same God, even the Father, is shewn forth, who fashioned man, and promised the inheritance to the fathers, who prepared it (?) for the resurrection of the righteous, and fulfils the promises for His Son's kingdom, afterward bestowing as a Father things which neither eye hath seen, nor ear heard, and which have not ascended into the heart of man. For One is the Son, who accomplished the Father's will ; and one the human race, in which the mysteries of God are accomplished, which angels desire to see, and have not power to explain the wisdom of God, through which the being which He fashioned is brought into conformity and concorporation with the Son ; that His offspring, the first begotten Word, might descend into the creature, that is into the being that [God] fashioned, and be received by

Him ; and that the creature again might receive the Word, and ascend up to Him, mounting above the angels, and come to be after the image and likeness of God."

LECTURE IV.

HIPPOLYTUS AND CLEMENT OF ALEXANDRIA.

IN Justin the Samaritan, who taught and who died a martyr's death at Rome, we have had before us the most characteristic of the Greek apologists of the second century, a man who went about clad only in the traditional philosopher's cloak, and who pleaded the cause of the Christians against the assaults of magistrates and populace on the ground that their faith and conduct should commend itself to philosophers and lovers of right reason.

In Irenæus, the disciple of Polycarp at Smyrna, who became bishop of Lyons and took an active part in promoting the peace of the Church when endangered by the intolerance of Victor, Bishop of Rome, we have had the first great theologian, in the strict sense of the

word, whose writings are to any great extent
preserved to us.   His great refutation of the
leading doctrines of the teachers called Gnostics,
is a still imperfectly worked mine of great
thoughts on God's dealings with mankind
through the ages, founded on the idea of the
Word before and after the Incarnation.

A few words are due to a disciple of Irenæus,
who forty years ago would have been commonly
reckoned an obscure and unimportant Father,
viz. Hippolytus.   Shortly after that date there
was published from a manuscript then lately
brought to Paris an elaborate Greek account
and refutation of early heresies, chiefly 'Gnostic,'
which it was soon recognised could not well have
any other author than Hippolytus.   There is no
real doubt about the matter, though, for quite
intelligible reasons, a few still hold otherwise.
The author writes as a bishop, and Hippolytus
is sometimes called Bishop of Rome, sometimes
bishop of Portus, the commercial port of Rome.
What he really was, is still an open question.
The most commonly received view is that which
was suggested by Döllinger, that for at least
a certain time Callistus and Hippolytus were
respectively recognised by different parties in

the Roman Church as each the only true and
lawful Bishop of Rome, though eventually Callistus alone was officially acknowledged as having
been bishop. The treatise itself is one of much
value for the extracts which it gives from Gnos-
tical writings. But of more general interest is
the narrative of some of the inner history of the
Roman Church under two successive bishops.
After every allowance has been made for the
partisanship of the writer, the picture is not an
agreeable one. But this lies outside our proper
subject. Of the part taken by Hippolytus it is
enough to say that he regarded Callistus and
the dominant authorities of the Roman Church
as dangerously lax in their admission of penitents to communion, and he likewise accused
them of favouring a doctrine not far from Sa-
bellianism, while he himself, from the manner in
which he expounded the doctrine of the Word, a
doctrine which evidently had little meaning for
them, was accused by them of setting up two
Gods to be worshipped. The end of the story
seems to be supplied by a curious early Roman
record which states that "Pontianus the bishop"
(the second after Callistus) and "Hippolytus the
presbyter were banished to Sardinia, to the

island of deadly climate." Perhaps, as has been suggested, the Roman magistrates took this way of enforcing peace in the Christian community, by getting rid of the two leaders together. From another record forming part of the same document we learn that the Roman Church in the middle of the fourth century kept on the same day the festival of Hippolytus in one cemetery and of Pontianus in another, both evidently as martyrs. Apparently they had both perished in the mines of Sardinia, and their bodies been received back in peace together. According to a somewhat confused tradition Hippolytus before his death had advised his followers to return to the communion of the Roman Church authorities. In the fourth and later centuries the strangest and most contradictory legends of his martyrdom became current. By a singular good fortune a contemporary memorial of him has been preserved, such as we possess for no other early Father whatever. Above three centuries ago a large part of an ancient sitting statue was dug up near Rome, and in due time recognised by the very interesting inscriptions on the base to have been no other than Hippolytus, though his name does not appear, and to have been erected

shortly after his death. In the great hall of the
Christian Museum at St John Lateran, as you
walk up between two lines of early Christian
sarcophagi of the highest interest for their
carving, you are faced by this great statue of
Hippolytus looking down upon you from the
platform at the end.

Hippolytus was one of the three most learned
Greek Fathers of his time, mostly the early part
of the third century. Of one of them Julius
Africanus, of whom only fragments remain, I
propose to say no more. To Origen we shall
come presently. Hippolytus' writings chiefly
fall under two heads, doctrinal treatises of a
controversial kind, and books connected with
the study of Scripture, either actual commentaries or essays at constructing some sort of
Scripture chronology. His defence of the Gospel
and Apocalypse of St John against certain contemporary gainsayers might be reckoned under
either head. He was especially interested in the
books of Daniel and Revelation, and in some of
the questions which they suggest. To him they
were by no means questions of idle curiosity ;
for in the new hostility of the Roman state, as
shewn in the persecution of Septimius Severus,

he supposed that he saw a fulfilment of Apo-
calyptic prophecy.   All that remains of him
however, with the exception of the great treatise
on heresies, itself far from complete, makes up
only a small volume.   This is the more remarkable as the fame of his writings spread far and
wide through the East, though the story of his
life was unknown outside Rome or else forgotten.

Hippolytus, following Irenæus, has conducted
us well into the third century.   We must now go
back half a generation or so to make acquaintance with a different region and a different way
of apprehending Christianity and its relation to
the world, though no doubt to a certain extent
anticipated by Justin Martyr.   Alexandria at
the mouth of the Nile had long been a special
home of Greek learning and philosophy, a place
where the culture of Egypt, Asia, and Europe
met together.   But of still greater moment was
the nature of the Judaism which had arisen in
the midst of the vast Jewish population of the
city, a Judaism almost wholly detached from the
legal influences which dominated the Judaism of
Palestine, and aiming especially at the comparison and harmonising of the Old Testament, and

specially the Pentateuch, with the better forms of Greek philosophy. Of this Græcised Judaism we have invaluable examples in Philo's writings. We know almost nothing of Alexandrian Christianity in its earlier days: but evidently it took its shape in no small degree from the type of Judaism which was already current in the place.

In the middle part of the second century we hear of a Christian Catechetical school at Alexandria, probably for the instruction of the highly educated converts who joined the Church. The second name preserved to us from the list of its heads or chief instructors is that of the Sicilian Pantænus, best remembered now as having gone on a missionary journey to India. Among his pupils was Clement of Alexandria, the Father who next claims our attention, and who often speaks of him, chiefly only under the title 'the elder,' with enthusiastic affection. Clement himself is said to have been an Athenian and probably was so. Profoundly Christian as he is, there is no Father who shews anything like the same familiarity with the ancient classical literature of Greece, especially the poetical literature. It is not clear whether he was of Christian or of

heathen parents: but we know from himself
that he travelled in early life, and came under
the influence of at least six different Christian
teachers in different lands, whom he calls
"blessed and truly memorable men." In Greece
he met the first, an Ionian, i.e. probably from
Western Asia Minor: two others in Magna
Græcia, the Greek-speaking South part of
Italy, one from Middle Syria and another
from Egypt. Whether he went to Rome, as
one would expect, does not appear: at all events
he refers to no teacher met there. From Italy
he crossed to the East, and there he learned
from an Assyrian, supposed to be Justin's scho-
lar Tatian, and from another, in Palestine, one
of Jewish birth. The last, he says, in order, but
virtually the first, he found lurking in Egypt, and
there he rested. He had found Pantænus. There
is reason to suppose that after a time he became
a colleague of Pantænus in the Catechetical
school, and at all events when Pantænus died
he succeeded him, probably somewhere about
the year 200. He was now or soon after a
presbyter of the Church. But two or three
years later through a change in the policy of
the Emperor Septimius Severus a persecution

broke out, which fell with much severity on
Alexandria; and the teachers of the Catechetical school, evidently including Clement, took
refuge elsewhere. A few years after this we
have a glimpse of him through a scrap of a
letter of his pupil Alexander, fortunately preserved by Eusebius. Alexander was at this
time apparently bishop of a Cappadocian church;
certainly he was in prison for conscience sake;
and he wrote a congratulatory letter out of his
prison on their recent choice of a new bishop,
sending it by Clement whom he calls "the blessed
presbyter, a man virtuous and well tried": who
by the Providence of God was then with him
and had stablished and increased the Church.
Clement cannot have lived much longer. In
another letter to Origen, written before 216,
Alexander again speaks affectionately of Clement as of Pantænus, both as now departed.
These testimonies are of value as shewing that
Clement's withdrawal from the approaching
persecution was due to no selfish cowardice,
but to such rightful avoidance of useless sacrifice of life as had been commanded by our
Lord Himself when He bade the Apostles
"When they persecute you in one city, flee

ye into another." For Alexander knew what martyrdom meant. He was made Bishop of Jerusalem under very peculiar circumstances, partly in consequence of what were regarded as Divine monitions, partly on account of what he had bravely endured in the persecution. It was the same to the end of his life. In the year 250 he was brought before the magistrates in the Decian persecution, and thrown into prison, and there he died.

Clement's chief writings form a connected series. First comes the Hortatory Address to the Greeks; the purpose is to shew that the Christian faith accomplishes what the heathen religions and philosophies vainly sought. It is too florid in style, and overloaded with superfluous illustrations. But it is inspired by the purest Christian fervour, and, apart from details, its general drift is at once lofty and true. Next comes the Παιδαγωγός or Tutor. The Tutor is not, as we might have guessed, the book itself; nor is he a man. It is none other than Christ the Word of the Father, the Tutor of mankind, educating them always in love and for their benefit, sometimes by gifts, sometimes by chastisements. The purpose of the book is the

guidance of the youthful convert from heathenism in habits belonging to Christian morality.
The heads of this morality are not vague
generalities, but practical and concrete enough ;
e.g. meat and drink, sumptuous furniture,
behaviour at feasts, laughter, bad language,
social behaviour, use of perfumes and garlands,
sleep, marriage duties, dress and ornaments, use
of cosmetics, use of baths, exercises. Alexandria seventeen centuries ago was clearly not so
very different a place from towns better known
to us. The permanent interest of these discus-
sions is very great. Often as we may have to
dissent from this or that remark, the wisdom
and largemindedness with which the Pædagogus
is written are above all praise. On the one
hand there is an all-pervading sense that the
Gospel is meant to be at once a moulding and a
restraining power in all the pettiest details as in
the greatest affairs of life : on the other hand
there is no morbid jealousy of the rightful use
of God's good gifts, and no addiction to restric-
tions not commanded by morality, or not re-
quired for self-discipline.

The third treatise of the series is commonly
known by the name στρωματεῖς (stroma*ta*,

common in modern books, is incorrect). A
στρωματεύς was a long bag of striped canvas,
in which bedclothes (στρώματα) were kept
rolled up. Various writers had used this name
for books of the nature of miscellanies. By
Clement it is in strictness used only of the seven
different books of the great treatise, Στρωματεύς
1, 2 etc. His descriptive title, if less quaint, is
more really interesting, " Gnostic jottings " (or
" notes ") " according to the true philosophy."
The Alexandrian convert from heathenism needed instruction not only in the outward behaviour
proper to the Christian life but also in the
deeper grounds of the Christian morality and
religion. In the schools of ordinary Greek
philosophy he would learn the value and the
dignity of wisdom and knowledge ; and now he
had to be taught that, whatever might be said
to the contrary by unwise Christians, these
things had a yet higher place under the Gospel :
for the Christ whom it proclaimed was not only
the Saviour of mankind in the simplest and
most obvious sense, but also One in whom lay
hid the treasures of wisdom and knowledge.
Clement was not made timorous by the associa-
tion of the word γνῶσις, ' knowledge,' with the

sects called heretical of those whom we now call
Gnostics.   Nay, it rather urged him to claim for
the Church a word and an idea which could not
be spared.   If St Paul had spoken of a Christian
Gnosis falsely so called, he had thereby implied
that there was a right Christian Gnosis, a Gnosis
truly so called ; and this is what Clement set
himself to defend and in part to provide.

It is a leading idea of Clement that the
Divinely ordained preparation for the Gospel
ran in two parallel lines, that of the Jewish Law
and Prophets and that of Greek philosophy.
His exposition of it is somewhat damaged by
his following an old but quite unfounded commonplace of Jewish apologetics, much repeated
by the Fathers, that the Greek philosophers
borrowed largely from the Old Testament.   But
the idea itself enabled him to look out both
on the past history of mankind and on the
mixed world around him with a hopeful and
helpful faith.   The treatise is a very discursive
one.   The leading heads are such as these :—
faith, Christian fear, love, repentance, endurance,
martyrdom, the true doctrine of marriage, teaching by signs and allegories, the attribution of
human feelings to God in Scripture.   There is

much comparison of Christian teaching on these themes with that of Greek philosophers and also of leading Pseudo-Gnostics, usually in a candid and discriminating manner.   But it is no merely theoretical knowledge that is here celebrated. The true Gnostic, according to Clement, is " he who imitates God in so far as is possible [for man] omitting nothing pertaining to such growth in the Divine likeness as comes within his reach, practising self-restraint, enduring, living justly, reigning over his passions, imparting of what he possesses, doing good by word and deed to the best of his power.   He, it is said, is greatest in the kingdom of heaven who shall do and teach in imitation of God by shewing free grace like His, for the bounties of God are for the common benefit[1]."

The fourth treatise of the series, written after Clement left Alexandria, was called Ὑποτυπώσεις, ' Outlines.'   The greater part of it unhappily is lost, though a fair number of difficult but peculiarly interesting fragments of it have been preserved.   Its subject was apparently fundamental doctrine, while it also contained expository notes on various books of the Bible,

_____

[1] Clem. Alex. *Strom.* II. p. 480 Potter.

including St Paul's Epistles and four out of the
Catholic Epistles.   What remains enables us to
see that this first great attempt to bring the
Gospel into close relation with the whole range
of human thought and experience on other lines
than those of the Pseudo-Gnostics contained, as
was natural, various theological crudities which
could not ultimately be accepted ; while it must
also have been rich in matter of permanent
value.

In addition to the great series of four, Clement wrote several minor treatises now almost
wholly lost, except a tract on the question
" What rich man can be saved ? "   It contains
the well-known beautiful story of St John and
the young man who became a bandit.

We must now bid farewell to Clement of
Alexandria.   He was not, as far as we know,
one of those whose writings have exercised a
wide or a powerful influence over subsequent
theology.   Large portions of his field of thought
remained for long ages unworked, or even
remain unworked still.   But what he at once
humbly and bravely attempted under great
disadvantages at the beginning of the third
century will have to be attempted afresh with

the added experience and knowledge of seventeen Christian centuries more, if the Christian faith is to hold its ground among men ; and when the attempt is made, not a few of his thoughts and words will probably shine out with new force, full of light for dealing with new problems.

A comparatively simple passage from the *Stromateis*[1] on faith, knowledge, love, will sufficiently illustrate his way of writing.

" Knowledge (i.e. Christian knowledge, Gnosis) is so to speak a perfecting of a man as a man, accomplished through acquaintance with Divine things, in demeanour and life and word, harmonious and concordant with itself and with the Divine Word. For by it faith is perfected, this being the only way in which the man who has faith becomes perfect. Now faith is a kind of inward good, and even without seeking God, it confesses that He is and glorifies Him as being. Hence a man must start from this faith, and when he has made increase in it must by the Grace of God receive as far as he can the knowledge (Gnosis) concerning Him....Not to doubt about God but to believe is the foundation of Gnosis, while Christ is both at once the

[1] Clem. Alex. *Strom.* VII. p. 864 P.

foundation and the structure built upon it, even
as through Him is both the beginning of things
and their [several] ends.   And the things that
stand first and last, I mean faith and love, do
not come by teaching ; but Gnosis transmitted
by tradition according to the Grace of God is
entrusted as a deposit to those who shew themselves worthy of the teaching ; and from Gnosis
the dignity of love shines forth, out of light into
light.   For it is said ' To him that hath shall
more be added '; to faith shall be added Gnosis,
and to Gnosis love, and to love the inheritance ";
i.e. (I suppose) the fulness of Divine Sonship.

I will only add half-a-dozen pregnant lines
from another Stromateus[1], expounding by a
memorable image the true relation between
man and God in prayer.   " As," he says, "men
attached at sea to an anchor by a tight cable,
when they pull at the anchor, draw not the
anchor to themselves but themselves to the
anchor, even so they who in the Gnostic life
draw God to them (i.e. so it seems to them) have
unawares been bringing themselves towards
God."

[1] Clem. Alex. *Strom.* IV. p. 633 P.

LECTURE V.

TERTULLIAN AND CYPRIAN.

THE last Father whose life and writings came before us was Clement of Alexandria. In him ancient Christian theology in some important respects reaches its highest point. There were after him greater as well as more influential theologians : but with all his very manifest defects there was no one whose vision of what the faith of Jesus Christ was intended to do for mankind was so full or so true.

His great pupil Origen, and one or two of Origen's own pupils, who worthily carried on the tradition of Alexandrian theology, will I hope come before us next time. Meanwhile we must turn aside to-day to a region geographically not remote from Egypt, but in other respects curiously unlike Egypt as regards the Christian theologians whom it bred in the earlier centuries.

The Roman proconsular province of Africa, approximately what we now in Church History for clearness' sake call " North Africa," was, as Mommsen has pointed out, a remarkably insulated region, being shut off from the interior and from the coasts to the East by vast deserts. The most important part of it answers roughly to the modern Tunis, Carthage being the capital. The Mediterranean divided it from Sicily and Italy: but there was close intercourse with Rome by water. Unhappily we know nothing of the foundation or earlier history of the North African Churches. But there is good reason to believe that they first created a Latin Bible. They also probably contributed largely to the creation of the church organisation which became prevalent in the West. They certainly created the distinctively Latin theology, which, developed especially by Augustine, and again by great theologians of the Middle Ages, and again by the leading Continental Reformers of the sixteenth century, has dominated men's thoughts in Western Europe respecting God and man, both for good and for evil. We have to consider to-day the first two great Fathers known to us from the North African Churches, probably the first two great Fathers whom they produced, Tertullian and Cyprian.

Nearly all that we know about Tertullian is gleaned from his own writings, and that is not much. He was probably born somewhere about the middle of the second century, and himself a native of North Africa. At Carthage he would have the fullest opportunity for acquiring the best culture of the time. Next to Rome, it was the second city of the Western Empire in size and importance; perhaps also, as Mommsen says, the most corrupt city of the West as well as the chief centre of the Latin cultivation and literature. Tertullian's writings shew what full use he made of these opportunities, as regards Greek and Roman literature. His occupation was that of an advocate; and the usual course of a lawyer's training in rhetoric would naturally lead him to spend some time at Athens and at Rome in youth. To an intelligent young lawyer Rome would be a very attractive place just then, on account of the distinguished Roman jurists of the time. All this time Tertullian was assuredly a heathen, and apparently a man of vicious life, as he states himself, and as the foulness which ever afterwards infested his mind too painfully confirms. How he became a Christian he never tells us directly: but it is tolerably clear that he is reciting his own experience when he more than once speaks of the moral impression produced on beholders by Christian martyrs. So in a famous passage of the *Apologeticum*[1] addressed to the heathen: " We multiply every time that we are mown down by you : the blood of Christians is seed....That very obstinacy which you reproach us with is a teacher. For who when he beholds it is not impelled to examine what are the inner contents of the matter ?" Again: " Every one looking on such endurance, smitten as with a kind of scruple, is both enkindled to examine whence it proceeds, and, when he has discovered, himself also at once follows the truth." Within the last few years it has become possible to surmise with some probability what the martyrdoms were which thus changed the course of Tertullian's life. We now know that the year 180, the first year of the Emperor Commodus, was the year when seven men and five women from the African town of Scilla were martyred at

---

[1] Tert. *Apol.* 50.

Carthage.   The Acts of their martyrdom are still extant[1].

Seventeen years later there was again persecution.   Apparently the Christians, or some Christians, refused to take part in the public festivities, probably involving idolatrous usages, which greeted the final victory of the Emperor Septimius Severus over other claimants of the imperial authority; and accordingly the existing laws seem to have been put in force against Christians, though probably not by the Emperor himself.   At least three of Tertullian's writings are memorials of this time ; his great *Apologeticum*, a brilliant and elaborate defence of Christians from the charges of all kinds brought against them, abounding in interesting matter of many kinds, and for its own purpose effective; yet all written with an exuberant cleverness which is too often merely painful.   This book was addressed to the governors of provinces, another the *Ad nationes* to the heathen peoples generally, a third *Ad martyres* to the Christian prisoners in North Africa.   To this crisis also belong the Acts of Martyrdom of Perpetua and

---

[1] See Lightfoot's *Apostolic Fathers* (2nd Edition), Ignatius, i. 524 foll.

Felicitas, which, if not written by Tertullian himself, as some think, at all events proceed from that set of North African Christians of which he was the leader, and shew clear signs of a Montanistic feeling. Of all the genuine Acts of Martyrdom that have been preserved to us these are the most interesting.

Taking a second leap of fourteen or fifteen years more, we come to another apologetic book of Tertullian's, addressed to the Proconsul Scapula. Severus had died at York in February 211, and persecution broke out afresh quite early in his successor Caracalla's reign. Thus we have Tertullian coming forward as an apologist at two distinct and distant crises.

But, if he was an energetic defender of the Church, he also became a hardly less energetic assailant of the Church. Jerome writes of him, "Till middle life he was a presbyter of the Church [this by the way is the only evidence we have, though it is probably sufficient, that Tertullian was ever more than a layman]; but," Jerome proceeds, "having afterwards fallen away to the doctrine of Montanus through the envy and contumelies of the clergy of the Roman Church, he refers to the new prophecy

in many books": Jerome then enumerates
certain books, now lost, which he calls specially
written against the Church.   The statement is
crude in form, and evidently coloured by reminiscences of Jerome's own quarrels with the
Roman clergy of a century and a half later:
but the substantial facts were probably to be
found in those books now lost.   There are
sufficient echoes of them in the existing books.
Every one must be struck by the parallelism
with the story of Hippolytus, all the more when
it is remembered that he and Tertullian were
contemporaries.   In more respects than one
they must have had strong mutual sympathies,
though Hippolytus, as far as we know, kept
clear of those special eccentricities which, as we
shall shortly see, were the fundamental cause of
Tertullian's eventual separation from the great
body of the Church.

The story which we have just been reading
carries us to what was doubtless the governing
interest of Tertullian's life, his relations to what
is called Montanism.   This, you will remember,
was an enthusiastic popular religious movement,
originating in the uplands of Phrygia.   It was
the erratic form taken by a great impulse

towards reformation which went through various churches late in the second century, partly due to a survival from an earlier stage of Christianity, but still essentially a reaction and an innovation. Briefly, its characteristics were these ; first, a strong faith in the Holy Spirit as the promised Paraclete, present as a heavenly power in the Church of the day ; secondly, specially a belief that the Holy Spirit was manifesting Himself supernaturally at that day through entranced prophets and prophetesses ; and thirdly, an inculcation of a specially stern and exacting standard of Christian morality and discipline on the strength of certain teachings of these prophets. An increase in the numbers and prosperity of the Church having brought an increase of laxity, it was not unnatural that attempts should be made to stem it by a rigorous system of prohibitions. To these three characteristics of Montanism may be added two others, fourthly, a tendency to set up prophets against bishops, the new episcopal organisation being probably favourable to that large inclu-siveness of Christian communion in which the Montanists saw only spiritual danger ; and fifthly, an eager anticipation of the Lord's

Second Coming as near at hand, and a conse-
quent indifference to ordinary human affairs.

Now it was the rigorous moral legalism of
Montanism that probably first attracted Tertullian. With a man of vehement and ill-disci-
plined character, as he was, and always remained,
conversion from heathenism might naturally be
accompanied by a violent rebound : and traces
of this are seen in what are apparently his
earliest writings; and then after a time we find
him drawn on from Montanist morality and
discipline to belief in the Montanist prophets,
and to the ecstatic type of inspiration which
they represented, and to their peculiar form of
devotion to the Paraclete. But all this time he
is simply a partisan within the Church, not in
any way separated from it. But there is a third
stage in which he writes clearly as the member
of a different body, claiming to be made up of
'men of the Spirit,' while he sneers at the
members of the great Church (the worldly
Church, he would say) as being only *psychici*,
'men of the soul.' In what manner he and his
'men of the Spirit' became finally detached
from the Church ; whether e.g. they seceded or
(more probably) were expelled, we do not know.

Personal squabbles, such as Jerome speaks of, may well have been mixed up with intolerances on either side, or on both. The time when this took place was probably some twenty years more or less from the beginning of the century. Jerome tells us that Tertullian is said to have lived to an extreme old age. This is all that we know.

Besides Tertullian's apologetic writings, nearly all of which have been already noticed, he was the author of a number of tracts of greater or less length addressed to Christians on various subjects belonging to morality or religion ; e.g. theatrical representations, idolatry (i.e. as mixed up with various trades and public occupations), the soldier's chaplet (the laurel crown which he held to be implicated in idolatry), flight in persecution, 'scorpiace' (martyrdom), prayer, patience, baptism, repentance, two books to his wife (against second marriage of women), adornment of women, exhortation to chastity (against second marriage of men), monogamy, modesty (Pudicitia, chiefly on the question of admitting penitents), fasting, against the Psychici, veiling of virgins, and the cloak (i.e. the philosopher's cloak, as now worn by Christians). Besides these

more or less practical writings, there are eight
or nine more of a strictly doctrinal character,
chiefly intended directly or indirectly for the
confutation of Pseudo-Gnostics or other supposed heretics ; but including a very important
treatise against Praxeas in which the doctrine
of the Trinity is defended against the Roman
Sabellians against whom Hippolytus wrote.
Three of the treatises bear the titles 'On the
Flesh of Christ,' 'On the Resurrection of the
Flesh,' 'On the Soul.'   Much the longest is the
treatise against Marcion in five books, probably
founded on earlier Greek writings.   In spite of
its reckless scurrility of tone, it contains many
passages both beautiful and true.   The most
popular however of all these doctrinal works,
and virtually a preface to them, is one entitled
'On the Prescription of Heretics.'   The main
drift of this most plausible and most mischievous
book is this: you try to argue with heretics and
to convince them, and you do no good : you
discuss Scripture with them and appeal to its
authority, and again you do no good : the only
way to overcome them is to shut them up
sharply with what the Roman law calls Prescription, and tell them *our* belief is the belief of the

Churches which trace back their origin to the
Apostles, and therefore it *must* be the true
belief. It was pardonable enough that Tertullian
should not have in mind the living growth of
belief which had been always going on in these
very churches. But it is another thing to find
him making war on all free action of the mind
and conscience in the things of faith, and
assuming that there are no depths of Divine
truth beyond the doctrines which men have
been able to formulate for public acceptance.
His complaint is not only against 'heretics' but
also against '*nostri*': he names no names, but
what he says seems specially directed against
Clement of Alexandria. It grieves him much
that an appeal is made to our Lord's words
"Seek and ye shall find, knock and it shall be
opened to you"; which he explains away by a
series of ingenuities, beginning with the assertions
that having been uttered early in our Lord's
ministry, while He was as yet imperfectly
known, they ceased to be true afterwards, and
that they were addressed to the Jews alone.

This is a sufficient illustration of Tertullian's
characteristic defects. To understand him
rightly we must remember that under the

Roman lawyer was probably hidden the man of Carthaginian i.e. the Phœnician blood. As in the case of Tatian, his utter want of sympathy with Greek and Roman greatness is probably due to the inborn sense of alien race. To the same source may perhaps be also traced his violence, his passion for bitter antagonisms. But it is a relief to read the touching words in which, writing on Patience, he bewails his own want of it. " It will be a kind of solace to dispute about that which it is not given me to enjoy, like sick men, who, since they are removed from health, do not know how to cease speaking about its advantages. So I poor wretch (miserrimus ego), always sick with the heats of impatience, must needs sigh after and call after and discourse about that health of patience which I fail to possess....Patience is so set at the head of the things of God, that no one can observe any precept, or perform any work well pleasing to the Lord, if he be a stranger to patience."

Apart from the infectiousness of his intolerance, Tertullian did serious injury to the Church of his own age and of later ages by beginning the process of casting the language of theology in the moulds supplied by the law courts. In

the Bible legal images take their place among
a variety of other images; but that is quite
another thing from the supremacy which legal
conceptions of spiritual things acquired through
the reckless use of legal phraseology.   But,
when the worst is said, Tertullian remains one
of the greatest of the Fathers, always needing
to be read with the utmost caution, but almost
always amply worth reading; not the less perhaps because it needs some labour to extract
the meaning from his closely condensed and
epigrammatic sentences.   He is a man of true
genius; and not that only but also a man of
warm and passionate Christian feeling; and
moreover one who, despite the obstacles created
by his own theories, had a keen eye for many
not obvious aspects of truth, which presented
themselves to him for the most part in sudden
flashes, and so by their frequent contradictions
reflect the moods of a fiery soul, itself always
full of contradictions.

As a sample of his more quiet controversial
vein, in which he is something much better than
controversial, we may take a few words of his on
the creation of man, in refutation of Marcion's
theory that the God of creation and of the

Law was only a just God, not a good God[1].
The exaggerations here and there do not
spoil the general drift. " Meanwhile the world
consisted of all good things, thereby sufficiently
shewing beforehand how much good was in store
for him for whom this whole [sum of things] was
being prepared.   Lastly, who could be worthy to
inhabit the works of God but His own image and
likeness?   That also was wrought by Goodness...
Goodness spoke [the words], Goodness fashioned
man out of slime into such a substance of flesh
built up into so many qualities out of one matter,
Goodness breathed [into him] making him a
soul that was living, not dead.   Goodness set
him to enjoy and reign over all things, and
moreover to give them names.   Goodness yet
further bestowed fresh enjoyment on man, that,
although a possessor of the whole world, he
should dwell in a specially pleasant region by
being shifted into Paradise, already out of a
world into a Church.   The same goodness provided also a help for him, that nothing good
might be wanting ; for it is not good, God said,
that man be alone: He knew that man would
profit by the sex of Mary and thenceforward of

[1] Tertullian *adv. Marc.* ii. 4.

the Church. [In this curious limitation the Montanist speaks.] But even the Law which thou blamest, which thou twistest into themes of controversy, it was Goodness that enacted it for the sake of man, that he might cleave to God, for fear he should seem not so much free as abandoned, on a level with his minions the other living creatures who had been cast loose by (from?) God and were free through His scorn of them; but that man alone might have the boast of having been alone worthy to receive a Law from God, and that, being a reasonable living creature with a capacity for understanding and knowledge, he might be held in likewise by that very liberty which belongs to reason, being subject to Him who had subjected to him all things. And in like manner it was Goodness that wrote on this law the counsel of observing it, 'In the day that ye eat thereof, ye shall surely die', for it graciously shewed the issue of transgression, for fear ignorance of the danger should help towards neglect of obedience....I call on thee therefore to recognise thus far the goodness of our God as shewn by works that were good, by blessings that were good, by acts of indulgence, by acts of Providence, by laws and forewarnings that were good and gracious."

Jerome tells us that once in North Italy he had met an old man who told him how when *he* was quite young he had in like manner seen at Rome a man of great age, formerly a notary of Cyprian's, and had heard from him how Cyprian was accustomed to pass no day without reading something of Tertullian's, and how he used often to say to him "Give me the Teacher," meaning Tertullian. This curious little reminiscence links together the two greatest men in the North African Church before Augustine. Strictly speaking Cyprian was not a theologian, while he was a great ecclesiastical ruler. His writings shew hardly any appropriation of the deeper elements in Tertullian's thoughts, those in which he claims affinity to Greek theology, perhaps partly due to borrowing from it : but the Roman legalism, which was so potent an ingredient in Tertullian's ways of thinking and speaking, acquired still greater force in its guidance of a man of simpler and more direct mind like Cyprian, accustomed through life to derive his thoughts of social order from the provincial administration of the Roman Empire, and when he had become a Christian bishop, writing almost always under the impulse of grave practical responsibilities. The depth and purity of his own religious feeling makes itself felt almost everywhere in his writings: yet the conceptions of the Church and its institutions which he sets forth, and which thenceforward dominated Latin Christianity, were indeed most natural under their circumstances of time and place, but not less truly involved injurious limitations and perversions of the full teaching of the Apostles.

We have the great good fortune of possessing a large amount of Cyprian's correspondence during the last ten years or so of his life, and also a memoir of him by his deacon Pontius. We have also from his pen about a dozen tracts on religious or disciplinary subjects. He bears well the testing of his inner self which these materials render possible. There is nothing petty and nothing ungoverned about him. He is always pursuing high ends according to the best of his lights with entire self devotion and seldom failing in patience and gentleness. He lived habitually in accordance with what he wrote in his early tract to his friend Donatus[1].

[1] Cypr. *ad Donat.* 4. 5.

"To God belongs whatever power we have. From that source we draw our life, from that source we draw our strength, from that source is taken and embraced the energy by which, while still placed here, we discern beforehand the signs of the things to come. Let only there be fear to guard innocence, that the Lord, who by the visitation of the heavenly mercy has graciously shone into our minds, may be held fast through righteous conduct as the guest of a mind that delights Him, lest the security thus received breed heedlessness and the old enemy steal in anew."..."The Spirit," he proceeds, "streams forth incessantly, overflows abundantly: let only our breast be athirst and open : as is [the measure] of faith to receive that we bring to it, such is [the measure] of inflowing grace that we drink in."

Cyprian was apparently converted to the Gospel in middle life. He was what we should call a country gentleman, and at the same time a man of good Latin education. Not long after he became a Christian he sold his estates, wholly or in part, to give the proceeds to the poor; though ultimately they were restored to him by the liberality of friends. Very early after his baptism he was admitted to the presbyterate,

and shortly afterwards, while still accounted a
neophyte, he was elected Bishop of Carthage.
He was evidently popular with the laity, with
whom the election seems to have chiefly rested.
His social position by itself could hardly have
won for him such a mark of confidence : doubtless he was already before his conversion known
as a man of virtuous life and high public spirit.
It was no light task that was laid on him by his
election.   Persecution had slumbered for about
a generation, and as a consequence various
abuses had sprung up in the Church, the bishops
and clergy not excepted.   But after a year and
a half came the persecution of Decius, the same
persecution in which, as we saw last week,
Alexander Bishop of Jerusalem perished in
prison.   Its fires were not without a purifying
effect on the Christian community : but it shortly
gave rise to a difficult question of discipline
which much exercised Cyprian, the treatment of
those who had " lapsed " or fallen away under
terror of death or torments.   On the one hand
there was a strong party of mere laxity at
Carthage, on the other a strong party of un-
swerving and indiscriminating severity at Rome ;
and the controversy was complicated by purely

personal elements, Cyprian's election not having been by any means universally acceptable. Of course it would be impossible to give now a narrative of the complicated transactions at Carthage and at Rome. It must suffice to say that Cyprian took an intermediate and carefully discriminative course, and that his policy was at last substantially adopted, though presently he was constrained by the force of circumstances, and especially a lesser persecution under Gallus, to accept a more indulgent set of rules than at first.

Presently North Africa was invaded by a terrible pestilence from the East which lasted on for long years afterwards. Cyprian instantly stood forward to organise his Christian flock for measures of help and relief, pecuniary and personal, insisting strongly on the duty of helping heathens as well as Christians in the spirit of true Sonship, following the example of Him who sends His rain and sunshine on all alike.

Presently a fresh controversy arose when Stephen became Bishop of Rome. The former controversy had left behind it an unhappy schism, the followers of Novatian having split off from the Church at large in the name of stricter discipline. The question now was whether persons having received Novatianist baptism, and subsequently joining the Church, needed to be baptised over again, or only to be received with laying on of hands. On this point Cyprian threw all his strength into the stricter theory, which had been falling into disuse in the West; and induced a large synod of North African Bishops to support it unanimously; while Stephen upheld the view that ultimately became fixed in the West, condemning such a repetition of baptism: only unfortunately he upheld it with much violence and intolerance.

Stephen died in August 257. In the same month a fresh persecution began under Valerian, and Cyprian was at once banished, though treated with remarkable respect and forbearance by the heathen authorities; and in his banishment he devoted himself to plans for help of other sufferers. But in about a year the persecution assumed a more terrible form. Xystus Bishop of Rome was beheaded as he sat preaching in his episcopal chair in one of the Roman cemeteries, and Cyprian returned to Carthage to await his now inevitable doom. The trial took place. The sentence was read "It is decreed that Thascius Cyprianus be executed by the sword." The record then proceeds "Cyprian the Bishop said, 'Thanks be to God'."

LECTURE VI.

ORIGEN.

IN the last two lectures the Fathers who have come before us have all belonged to Africa. It will be the same to-day. We return now from North Africa, and the two great Fathers whom at this early time it brought forth for Latin theology, to Egypt and to the most characteristically Greek theology.

If the influence of Clement of Alexandria over the later times of early Christianity was less than we might have expected, the same cannot be said of his great pupil Origen. Not only had he the veneration of devoted disciples for several generations; but the theologies built up in the succeeding centuries of the age of the Fathers would, as far as we can see, have been very different from what they actually were, had

it not been for the foundations laid by him.
Above all, his influence as an interpreter of the
Bible, direct and indirect, has been both wide
and lasting. In the ancient Church three men
stand out above all others as having left a deep
mark by their independent interpretation of
Scripture. The other two are Theodore of
Mopsuestia (late in the fourth century), the
highest representative of the School of Antioch,
and (a generation later) Augustine the North
African, the primary teacher of the Latin West.
Not the least interesting fact however in the
history of the influence of Origen as an interpreter is the way in which his thoughts and
often his words were appropriated and handed
on by Latin Fathers, and especially the three
greatest Latin Fathers of the fourth century,
Hilary of Poitiers (theologically the greatest of
them all), Ambrose and Jerome. In this manner,
as well as by direct translations of some of
Origen's works, Origenian ideas, penetrating
down through various channels, supplied a by no
means insignificant element in the very miscel-
laneous body of traditional interpretation which
prevailed till the fresh and open study of the
meaning of Scripture was restored, chiefly by

the Revivers of learning just before the Reformation and by some of the Reformers themselves. The permanent value of his interpretation of Scripture is much lessened by the fact
that, in common with most ancient interpreters
outside the School of Antioch, he shews an
excessive devotion to allegorical senses: yet
along with this mere fancifulness we find in him
evidence of a genuine and profound study of the
words of Scripture. For all his great and lasting
influence, Origen's name has been by no means
surrounded with the halo of conventional glory
which has traditionally adorned Fathers inferior
to him in every way. Some of his speculations
were doubtless crude and unsatisfactory: but
these are but trifles beside the vast services which
he rendered to theology ; and accordingly, every
now and then, from Athanasius onwards, he has
received cordial words of vindication from men
who were able to recognise goodness and greatness, in spite of an unpopular name.

Unlike the Fathers whom we have been
lately considering, Clement of Alexandria, Tertullian, Cyprian, Origen had the blessing of
Christian parentage, and received from his father
Leonides a careful education both in the ordinary

Greek culture of the day and in the study of
Scripture, becoming the pupil of Clement. He
was not seventeen when that persecution of
about the year 202 under Septimius Severus
occurred which drove Clement from Alexandria,
and Leonides was thrown into prison. Origen
himself, being restrained by a device of his
mother's from rushing to join him in the anticipated martyrdom, wrote to him entreating that
no care for his family should be allowed to shake
his constancy. On his father's martyrdom, with
confiscation of goods, he provided for his own and
his mother's and six brothers' wants by teaching,
except that he was lodged by a lady of wealth.
Some heathens came to him for instruction,
including Plutarchus, who was martyred, and
Heraclas, who became Bishop of Alexandria;
and thus he was led to take up, though in an
informal way, the dropped work of the Catechetical School. After a time he was placed
formally at its head by the Bishop Demetrius.
For some twelve years he went on without other
interruption than a short visit to Rome and
another to Arabia, lecturing to large audiences
as a layman, living a sternly rigorous and self-
denying life. To this time belongs the rash act

of self-mutilation always associated with his name, suggested to him by a misunderstanding of the real drift of one of our Lord's sayings. Meanwhile he laboured to fit himself for his work more and more. On the one hand he studied Hebrew ; on the other he attended the lectures of the most eminent heathen philosophers, that he might be ' better able to understand the thoughts of those ' who came to him for help. The work increased so much that he associated with himself his convert Heraclas.

At length about the year 215 he was driven by tumults to leave Alexandria, as Clement had done, and took refuge for a considerable time at Cæsarea, the Greek or Roman capital of Palestine. Alexander, now Bishop of Jerusalem, of whom we heard a fortnight ago, and the Bishop of Cæsarea joined in inviting him to preach (ὁμιλεῖν) to the assembled congregation. On receiving a remonstrance from Demetrius at their permitting a layman to preach before bishops, they cited various precedents in defence of their action. But Demetrius refused to give way, and fetched Origen back to Alexandria in a peremptory way. After his return he was persuaded by Ambrosius, now a friend, formerly

a convert of his from some Pseudo-Gnostic sect,
to undertake commentaries in writing, for which
purpose Ambrosius provided short-hand writers.

But after Origen had taught at Alexandria
for about a quarter of a century, his career there
came to a painful end.   The Churches of Achaia,
being much distracted by what were called
heresies (of what kind, is not related), invited
him to come to their help.   He started without
obtaining license from Demetrius (but under
what circumstances we do not know), and took
his way through Palestine.   There he was
ordained presbyter by the Bishop of Cæsarea,
with Alexander's knowledge and approval.
He then completed his journey to Greece,
making sojourns at Ephesus and Athens, and
at length returned home.   His reception there
is a sad one to read of.   Demetrius assembled
"a synod of bishops and of certain presbyters,"
by whom he was forbidden to teach or even
reside in Alexandria.   They did not agree to
reject his ordination, as apparently Demetrius
wished: but this too he obtained from a
subsequent smaller meeting of bishops alone.
Our too fragmentary authorities do not tell
us quite clearly the ground of condem-

nation.   Apparently it was the ordination
of one who was mutilated, though it is also
possible that doctrinal differences and it may be
even personal jealousies were unavowed motives
of action.   There is reason to believe that the
Roman Church supported the action of Demetrius ; but it was entirely ignored by the Bishops
of Asia ; those of Palestine, Arabia, Phœnicia
(i.e. probably North Syria) and Achaia being
specially mentioned.   Origen left Alexandria
for ever, and though beloved disciples of his own
succeeded Demetrius as bishop, apparently no
attempt was made to undo the banishment.
Gentlest, humblest, and most peace-loving of
men, Origen would be the last to disturb the
peace of the Church for his own sake.

Accordingly for the third time he betook
himself to the friendly Cæsarea, and there in the
great seaport beside the Mediterranean he made
his permanent home for the rest of his life, above
twenty years.   Being welcomed and cherished
by the two Palestinian Bishops of whom we
heard before, he carried on his literary work as
a Christian theologian with the help of Ambrosius, and at the same time resumed oral
instruction, partly by expository sermons of a

comparatively simple kind in Church, partly by
more advanced lectures to students and philo-
sophical enquirers, as at the Catechetical School
of Alexandria.

With this period are specially connected the
names of two illustrious disciples, Firmilianus
and Gregory of Neocæsarea. Firmilianus was
apparently already bishop of the Cappadocian
Cæsarea, the capital of the inland regions of
Eastern Asia Minor, when this recorded intercourse with Origen took place, though it may
well have begun at an earlier time. Sometimes
he used to get Origen to come to visit him in
Cappadocia to instruct his Churches ; sometimes
he used to make stays in Palestine to have the
personal benefit of hearing Origen discourse. A
man of still greater eminence in the years after
the middle of the third century was Gregory
Bishop of Neocæsarea in Pontus. According to
his own narrative he had travelled to Palestine
to educate himself as an advocate by study at
Beirût, where there was a famous School of
Roman Law; but before fixing himself there,
he had travelled on to Cæsarea with his sister,
whose husband held an official post there.
Beirût however was soon given up. He fell

(with his brother) under the spell of Origen's teaching and personal presence, and remained under his instruction for five years. On his departure he delivered an address in expression of his gratitude, and this address is still extant. In it he describes how he first came under Origen, and how Origen dealt with him and with other pupils. First came a training in the faculties of the mind, a pruning away of wild growths of opinion for opinion's sake, an enforcement of clear thinking and exact speaking. Then came the study of the visible order of nature, founded on the study of geometry. Thirdly, came Christian ethics as founded on godliness, which he called the beginning and the end of all the virtues. Having passed through these preliminary stages of mental discipline, Origen's pupils were encouraged to read freely in the works of Greek poets and philosophers, and then, thus prepared, to enter on the study of Christian theology proper, more especially in its primary source, the Bible.

Such was the method of Origen's regular teaching at Cæsarea. But he did not refuse invitations to leave home for a while, and give help to other Churches. Some time, we know,

he spent at Athens. Twice he was asked to
come into Arabia to help in neutralising false
doctrines which had arisen there. In each case,
instead of using declamation and anathemas, he
sought quiet conference with the men who had
propounded these doctrines ; and in each case
succeeded in persuading them that they had
been in error. If later controversies had been
dealt with in the same spirit, what a different
Christendom and a different world would now
be meeting our eyes !

Our first glimpse of Origen was as a boy,
encouraging his father to face martyrdom without hesitation, undistracted by any anxieties for
his helpless family. A third of a century later
a similar task fell to his lot. The emperor
Alexander Severus, who had been friendly to
the Christians, and with whose mother Mamæa
Origen had had some intercourse, had come to
a violent end, and his murderer and successor
Maximinus entered on a persecution of such
Christians, it would seem, as had stood in
special favour with Alexander. Origen was
apparently saved by a Christian Cappadocian
lady, Juliana, who kept him out of harm's way.
But Ambrosius and a presbyter of Cæsarea were

imprisoned, and to them Origen wrote an Exhortation which we still possess.

But fifteen years later, or less, he had to suffer grievously in his own person. In that persecution of Decius in which his old fellow-student and supporter Alexander died in prison, he too was cast into prison, and had to undergo a succession of tortures. Decius' reign was a short one; and on his death Origen was released from prison, shattered by the treatment which he had received, and two years later he died at Tyre, being not far from 70 years of age. His tomb in the Cathedral of Tyre is several times in the early Middle Ages noticed as then still visible, and the inscription of it still later; and a tradition of his place of burial is still said to be current in the neighbourhood. Though he does not bear the conventional title of Saint, no saintlier man is to be found in the long line of ancient Fathers of the Church.

One of the best known sentences of Butler's Analogy, occurring in the Introduction, is to this effect: "Hence, namely from analogical reasoning, Origen has with singular sagacity observed, that *he who believes the Scripture to have proceeded from him who is the Author of*

Nature, may well expect to find the same sort of difficulties in it, as are found in the constitution of Nature." These few words are characteristic of the subjects of Origen's writings. He was deeply and reverently occupied in meditation on all things in heaven and earth of which the human mind can take any cognisance ; but the Bible was the centre of all his thoughts and of all his studies. He wrote commentaries or preached homilies, taken down by rapid writers, on a large proportion of books of both Testaments. What is lost was far more than what is preserved: but we still have much, large portions of the commentaries on St Matthew and St John, that on the Romans in a too free Latin condensed translation, some Homilies on Jeremiah, many Greek fragments on various books, and many Latin translations of Homilies, chiefly on the Old Testament. A biblical work of another kind was what is called Origen's Hexapla, an arrangement of the books of the Old Testament in (for the most part) six parallel columns, each containing a distinct text, the Hebrew, the same in Greek letters, the Septuagint, and three other Greek translations. Numerous detached readings copied from it have been preserved, but hardly more. By this combination of texts Origen hoped to throw light on the meaning of many passages in which a Greek reader would be either bewildered or misled if he had only the Septuagint before him. Besides the *Exhortation to Martyrdom* mentioned before, we possess a very interesting little treatise of Origen's on Prayer. Very little unhappily remains of his letters, of which a collection was made some time after his death. But we fortunately possess in one shape or other what were probably his two greatest works, the systematic doctrinal treatise on *First Principles*, written before his departure from Alexandria, preserved for the most part only in a too free Latin version; and the eight books against Celsus in the original Greek, written near the end of his life. In connexion with Origen's writings it is worth while to mention the *Philocalia*, a small collection of extracts from them chiefly bearing on the interpretation of Scripture, made late in the fourth century by Basil and Gregory of Nazianza. It was from this source that Butler made his quotation, and the little book deserves to be better known.

As an easy specimen of the book on First

Principles, which chiefly consists of somewhat
difficult speculative meditations, we may take
a passage on the thirst for Divine knowledge
implanted in the heart of man, and, however
little he may know in this life, intended to
render him capable of even higher levels of
knowledge in the stages of the future life.

"Therefore, as in those crafts which are
accomplished by hand, we can perceive by our
understanding the reason which determines what
a thing is to be, how it is to be made and for
what purposes, while the actual work is accomplished by the service of the hands; so in the
works of God which are wrought by His own
hand, we must understand that the reason and
designs of the things which we see made by
Him, remain unseen. And just as, when our
eye has seen things made by the craftsman, the
mind, on observing something made with especial
skill, is forthwith anxious to enquire in what
fashion or manner or for what purposes the
thing has been made; so much more and in an
incomparably higher degree the mind is anxious
with an unspeakable longing to recognise the
reason of the things which we behold made by
God. This longing, this ardent desire, has we

believe without doubt been implanted in us by God : and, just as the eye naturally requires light and object of vision, and our body by nature demands food and drink, so our intellect is possessed with a fit and natural desire for knowing the truth of God and discovering the causes of things. Now this desire we have received from God not in order that it should never be satisfied or be capable of satisfaction : otherwise vainly will the love of truth appear to have been implanted in our intellect by God the Creator, if it is made never capable of satisfying its longing. Wherefore even in this life those who have laboriously given their attention to godly and religious meditations, even though they obtain but a small amount from the great and infinite treasures of the Divine wisdom, yet just because they keep their minds and attention turned towards these subjects and outstrip themselves in this desire, receive much profit from the very fact that they are directing their minds to the search and love of discovering truth and making them more ready to receive future instruction : just as, when a man wishes to paint a portrait, if a pencil sketch in bare outline first marks out the plan of the coming picture, and pre-

pares marks on which the features may be laid, the
rough outline doubtless is found more ready to
receive the true colours ; so may a mere sketch,
a rough outline by the pencil of our Lord Jesus
Christ, be traced on the tablets of our heart.
And perhaps it is for this reason that it is said,
'For to everyone that hath shall it be given,
and it shall be added to him.' Whence it is
certain that to those who possess in this life a
sort of rough outline of truth and knowledge
shall be added in the future the beauty of the
perfect picture. Such, I imagine, was the desire
indicated by him who said 'But I am constrained in two ways, having a desire to depart
and be with Christ, for it is far better'; knowing
that when he had returned to Christ, he would
recognise more clearly the reasons of all things
which are done on earth[1]."

The Books against Celsus contain at once
the best and the most comprehensive defence of
the Christian faith which has come down to us
from the days of the Fathers. They defend
it not against popular prejudice and malice
only, as the early Apologists had done, but
against the careful and powerful indictment laid

---

[1] Origen, ii. IV. p. 236.   Redep. (ii. XI. 4, 5).

by an earnest though scoffing heathen philosopher who was also apparently an accomplished
Roman lawyer, writing in the name of the
highest philosophy of the time, and passionately
devoted to the welfare of the Roman Empire.
A long time had passed between the writing
of Celsus' "True Account," as he called his
literary onslaught on the Christians and their
faith, and its coming into Origen's hands.   He
had no real knowledge about the author, but he
evidently felt that if he could answer *him*
successfully, he would practically have effectu-
ally upheld the cause of the Gospel at all points.
If he sometimes fails to understand on what this
or that smart saying of Celsus' really rested, he
never shows the unfairness of the mere partisan.
The candour and patience of his treatise are
among its brightest qualities.

The whole treatise amply repays reading and
re-reading: one passage however must now
suffice.   It is the reply to Celsus' scoff about
the lateness of the Incarnation and its limitation
to an obscure corner of the world, a scoff in form,
but covering a serious question.   As regards the
time, Celsus compared it to the comic poet's
representation of Zeus as waking out of sleep

and suddenly sending Hermes to men. As regards the place, he asked why God did not breathe souls into many bodies, and send them all over the earth.   Here is the answer.

"Observe here too Celsus' want of reverence when he most unphilosophically brings in a comic poet, whose object is to raise a laugh, and compares our God the Creator of the Universe with the god in his play who on awaking despatches Hermes. We have said above that, when God sent Jesus to the human race, it was not as though He had just awoken from a long sleep, but Jesus, though He has only now for worthy reasons fulfilled the divine plan of His incarnation, has at all times been doing good to the human race. For no noble deed among men has ever been done without the Divine Word visiting the souls of those who even for a brief space were able to receive such operations of the Divine Word. Nay even the appearance of Jesus in one corner of the world (as it seems) has been brought about for a worthy reason: since it was necessary that He of whom the prophets spoke should appear among those who had learnt one God, who read His prophets and recognised Christ preached in them, and that He

should appear at a time when the Word was
about to be diffused from one corner to the
whole world.

"Wherefore also there was no need that many
bodies should be made everywhere, and many
spirits like to that of Jesus, in order that the
whole world of men might be illumined by the
Word of God. For it sufficed that the one
Word rising like the Sun of Righteousness from
Judæa should send forth His speedy rays into
the soul of them that were willing to receive
Him. And if anyone does wish to see many
bodies filled with a divine Spirit, ministering like
Him the one Christ to the salvation of men in
every place, let him take note of those who in
all places do honestly and with an upright life
teach the word of Jesus, who are themselves
too called 'Christs' ('anointed ones') in the
passage 'Touch not mine anointed ones and do
my prophets no harm.' For even as we have
heard that antichrist comes and nevertheless
have learnt that there are many antichrists in
the world, even so, when we recognise that
Christ has come, we observe that owing to Him
many Christs have been born in the world, to
wit all those that like Him have loved righteous-

ness and hated iniquity: and for this reason
God, the God of Christ, anointed them too with
the oil of gladness. But He however, having
loved righteousness and hated iniquity to a
higher degree than those who are His partners, .
has also received the first-fruits of the anointing,
and, if we may so term it, has received the
entire unction of the oil of gladness: while they
that were His partners partook also in His
unction each according to his capacity.

"Wherefore, since Christ is the head of the
Church, so that Christ and His Church are one
body, the ointment has descended from the head
to the beard (the symbol of the full-grown man
Aaron), and this ointment in its descent reached
to the skirts of his clothing. This is my answer
to Celsus' impious speech when he says that
'God ought to have breathed His Spirit into
many bodies in like manner and to have sent
them forth throughout the world.' So then
while the comic poet to raise a laugh has
represented Zeus as asleep and as waking up
and sending Hermes to the Greeks, let the
Word which knows that the nature of God is
sleepless teach us that God with regard to
seasons orders the affairs of the world as reason

demands. But it is not to be wondered at, if,
seeing that the judgments of God are sublime
and hard to interpret, uninstructed souls do err,
and Celsus among them.

"There is then nothing absurd in the fact that
to the Jews, with whom were the prophets, the
Son of God was sent; so that beginning with
them in bodily form He might arise in power
and spirit upon a world of souls desiring to be
no longer bereft of God[1]."

At Origen's death in the year 253 we are
still nearly half a century from the end of the
first three centuries, and nearly three-quarters of
a century from the Council of Nicæa. If time
permitted, it would not be difficult to give some
account of Fathers belonging to this interval
who are quite worthy of being known. At the
same time it is true that we have only fragments,
sometimes hardly that, of the men who seem as
if they had been best worth knowing. Moreover, with the exception of the almost forgotten
Lucianus of Antioch, they seem to have been
less original and important Fathers than nearly
all those who have come before us this term.
The most attractive group is formed by the

[1] Origen adv. Celsum, vi. 78 foll.

disciples of Origen, not only the two already spoken of, but Heraclas, and Pierius, and Dionysius of Alexandria of whom we can obtain a tolerably vivid and very pleasant image from the fragments of his letters preserved by Eusebius, shewing how a great bishop trained by Origen would deal with the difficult questions raised by persecution without and false doctrine within. Then would come Pamphilus, the loving collector of memorials of Origen and zealous champion of his good name against the detractors who were beginning to assail it; himself a martyr in the terrible last persecution at the beginning of the fourth century. And Pamphilus in turn leads to his younger friend Eusebius the historian, who lived and wrote in the fourth century, and yet might in some ways be called the last of the Ante-Nicene Fathers.

But we must be content with this very hurried glance at that most important but most obscure time between the death of Origen and Cyprian and the Council of Nicæa. A better break than at the death of Origen we could hardly desire. Not to speak of the men of later days, looking only at those other Fathers who have come before us this term, we cannot help

recognising that they had often work given them
to do which he could not do; and that they
were enabled to see some truths which he could
not see. But he is for us practically the last and
most characteristic of the early Fathers, properly
so called, the Fathers who lived while Christian
thought could still be free, and while Christian
faith still embraced the whole world. From all
these early Fathers taken together, you will, I
trust, have gained the feeling, if you had it not
already, that Christian pastors and teachers in
this nineteenth century can ill afford to neglect
the thoughts and aspirations of those earliest
Christian ages, though, like the thoughts and
aspirations of all intervening times, they must
remain a dead letter to us till they are interpreted by the thoughts and aspirations of our
own time as shone upon by the light of the
Spirit who is the teacher of Christ's disciples in
every succeeding age.